Praise for *Prosperity*

"Beautifully written from the heart and soul."

—Howard Wong, Vice President,
Connor, Clark & Lunn Private Capital Ltd.

"Brain's philosophy, as captured by the essays in this book, is a gift to our industry. As was the case for myself, it will become the tipping point to success for many advisors around the world. By reading this book, and reflecting on its message, you will learn to challenge the modern financial industry's impulsive nature, replacing it with the strength of calm optimism, protective instincts, and purpose-driven decisions."

—Meagan S. Balaneski, CFP, R.F.P., CLU,
Presidents Award Recipient, Financial Planning Standards Council;
CEO, Advantage Investment and Insurance Advisors

"I've gotten to know Brad Brain quite well over the last ten years and the one thing that has never changed is his obsession with discovering and sharing financial truth. Once you've read this book, you will wonder how on earth some people still go through life without a proper financial plan and without a financial advisor who truly sits at their side of the table."

Richard Vetter, BA, CFP, CLU, ChFC
President, WealthSmart Incorporated

"Brad does an excellent job of explaining the realities of the financial markets. This book is a must read, and will help make complicated financial matters easy to understand."

Jas Gill, MBA, CFP, CIM, CLU
Vice President, Sales and Marketing
IDC Worldsource Insurance Network

It all comes down
to making decisions
that are consistent
with your objectives
& keeping your focus
when things get stormy.

You are in good hands
with Melanie & Kevin!

All the best,

PROSPERITY

Making Smart, Strategic
Decisions about Money

BRAD BRAIN, CFP, R.F.P., CLU, CH.F.C, CHS, CIM, FCSI, TEP

Brad Brain Financial Planning Inc.
Fort St. John, British Columbia

Prosperity: Making Smart, Strategic Decisions About Money
Copyright © 2017 by Brad Brain

Brad Brain Financial Planning Inc.
Fort St. John, BC, Canada
1 250 785 1655
bradbrainfinancial.com
brad@bradbrainfinancal.com

Printed in Canada

Book design: Carla Green, Clarity Designworks
Cover and interior artwork: Barbara Daley, 7 Bangles Art & Design

ISBN 978-0-9959451-0-4

Financial Advisors and Industry Participants
Quantity discounts are available for purchases of 20 or more copies. Copies of *Prosperity* can also be included in combination with speaking engagements. Contact Brad Brain at brad@bradbrainfinancial.com or 1 250 785 1655 to make arrangements.

Industry Disclaimer
At the time of publication, Brad Brain is an Investment Advisor of Aligned Capital Partners Inc. (ACPI). ACPI is a member of the Investment Regulatory Organization of Canada (IIROC) and the Canadian Investor Protection Fund (CIPF). The opinions expressed are those of the author and not necessarily those of ACPI. Brad Brain also offers financial planning services and is licensed for the sale of life insurance products. Brad Brain is registered through separate organizations for each service offered. This publication is a collection of essays written by the author between 1999 and 2014. While content accuracy has been verified where possible, Brad Brain was not an agent of ACPI during this period.

The opinions expressed by the author are not intended as and should not be interpreted as personalized advice including, without limitation, investment, financial, legal, accounting, or tax advice. It is recommended that the reader treat the information contained as general in nature and consider getting advice from an appropriate professional.

For my precious children,
Emily Verushka Brain and William Vladimir Clinton Brain

If you can fill the unforgiving minute
With sixty seconds' worth of distance run,
Yours is the Earth and everything that's in it,
And – which is more – you'll be a Man, my son!
RUDYARD KIPLING

Contents

Foreword

THIS IS A COLLECTION of essays that I have written over many years, through all kinds of market conditions. While the anecdotes may be historical, the wisdom is timeless. You may see some chapters have similar themes, even though the essays may have been written years apart. Real truth doesn't change over time, and the fundamental messages of this anthology are immutable.

I wrote this book as the antithesis to the transitory and sensationalistic works that are commonly found. We live in an age where information is everywhere, but knowledge is scarce. We are now in the world of the 24 hour news cycle; one that predominantly focuses on a cult of market timing and selection. We give abundant attention to things of little lasting significance, yet, paradoxically, ignore matters of great importance.

This book is different than some. I am not a journalist, and I don't have a get rich quick scheme. I am a professional financial advisor. What I do have is plain language wisdom that comes from two decades of advising everyday Canadians about making smart decisions with their money. I believe the biggest value I can add to my clients is saving them from making the big mistake.

It all comes down to this: focusing on making smart decisions that are consistent with what truly and uniquely matters to you. That's the proven way to achieve your own prosperity.

—Brad Brain, February, 2017

PART ONE

Just Change the Channel

What do you do when the narrative is no longer beneficial? Just change the channel.

■ ■ ■ ■ ■ ■

Financial Pornography

YESTERDAY I WAS LOOKING for some information on the Internet, and I ended up watching a few video clips from one of these business news channels. This is unusual for me.

When I say unusual I'm not referring to researching stuff – I usually spend about 2 hours a day reading. I'm referring to giving any attention whatsoever to the business news channel. Which is interesting when you think of it. I spend about 2 hours a day on research, and I never watch the business news.

Why would that be? Simple, really. For the most part, the business news channels are nothing more than financial pornography.

I know that these types of programs have their loyal followings, but the simple truth is that a bunch of self-proclaimed gurus sitting around giving 30-second sound bites on which direction the market is going in the next five minutes is nothing more than a tawdry, often lurid, way of getting your attention. It's not wisdom; it's the professional wrestling of the business world.

The term financial pornography has been around for a decade or so, but it's still rather loosely defined. Paraphrasing my dictionary's definition of the word pornography, one could say it means the sensational depiction of behaviour designed primarily to cause excitement.

Financial porn is everywhere. Here are some catchy phrases from a story that I read just this morning: "The latest turn in the expanding spiral of trouble for financial markets, one that won't go away just because investors stuck their heads in the sand for a day" and "in the current environment, that's the business equivalent of playing road hockey on a freeway" and, in reference to some potentially optimistic developments, "those were just a couple of nice-looking trees in a burning forest."

Geez, does it sound like a sensational depiction of behaviour designed primarily to cause excitement? Ya think?

Financial porn is not random, nor coincidental, nor accidental. It is completely intentional, but you don't need to simply take my word for it.

In an article entitled "Confessions of a Former Mutual Funds Reporter" that appeared in the April 26, 1999 issue of Fortune Magazine, the anonymous author, who works for the very same Fortune magazine, writes, "Mutual funds reporters lead a secret investing life. By day we write "Six Funds to Buy NOW!" We seem to delight in dangerous sectors like technology. We appear fascinated with one-week returns. By night, however, we invest in sensible index funds."

"I know, because I once was one of those reporters--condemned to write a new fund story every day--when I covered funds for an online publication. I was ignorant. My only personal experience had been bumbling into a load fund until a colleague steered me to an S&P 500 index fund."

"I worried I'd misdirect readers, but I was assured that in personal-finance journalism it doesn't matter if the advice turns out to be right, as long as it's logical. You're supposed to produce the most stories "that end in investment decisions," so publications substitute formulas for wisdom. The formula for recommending funds: Filter according to returns, then add something trendy."

"The problem is that recent returns, whether from one week or the old standby three years, don't predict future results. Nothing predicts future results. The best you can do is to hold on to low-cost, diversified funds and be oblivious to short-term static."

"We did tell people that. But we were preaching buy-and-hold marriage while implicitly endorsing hot-fund promiscuity. The better we understood the industry, the sillier our stories seemed. When a certain colleague would see a rival publication with its obligatory SIX FUNDS TO BUY NOW! headline, he would slap the magazine down on his desk and protest with feigned jealousy, "We were scooped! They stole our story!"

"Unfortunately, rational, pro-index-fund stories don't sell magazines, cause hits on Websites, or boost Nielsen ratings. So rest assured: You'll keep on seeing those enticing but worthless SIX FUNDS TO BUY NOW! headlines as long as there are personal-finance media."

You see, the thing about this is that if you are a talking head on a business news network the name of the game isn't being accurate. It's all about getting your attention, and there really is no downside to being wrong.

So they can fire away with melodramatic phrases like "those were just a couple of nice-looking trees in a burning forest" and call it reporting the news. They can write articles titled "Six Funds to Buy NOW!" and call it timely and reasoned advice.

From that perspective, all the better to pump out liberal doses of financial porn, since the objective is not to be accurate as much as it is to be entertaining. Be dramatic. Be flamboyant. Be wrong even. Just don't be boring.

The problem is that a sensational depiction of behaviour designed primarily to cause excitement can put the reader in a bad state of mind for making smart financial decisions. And, although some financial pornography is benign, unfortunately some of it isn't.

If you see stuff like "Get your money out of your Registered Retirement Savings Plan tax-free" or "Get a $10,000 tax deduction with a $2000 charitable donation" or "Make 60% returns guaranteed with off-shore investments", please recognize this for what it is.

Meanwhile, as my friends at Brandes Investment Partners say, "We take a long-term perspective, and believe that no, or very little, short-term 'market news' provides useful information to value investors."

from December 2007

■ ■ ■ ■ ■ ■

The Worst Plunge in Years

IN LATE JULY North American stock markets suffered the worst decline in years. Or did they?

I don't mean to say that the markets didn't come down. They did. What I mean is, was it really the worst downturn in years? Well, yes and no. And it's mostly no.

Here's the thing about the financial news – for most people it is really boring stuff. And that's a bit of a problem for the people in the business of reporting financial news.

Boring stuff doesn't get people's attention, and the media needs to have people's attention in order to attract advertisers. And, at the end of the day, the name of the game is selling advertising.

So how do you get people's attention? Well, dramatic phrases like "the worst plunge in years" are a good start.

Check it out for yourself. Make a note of where the Toronto Stock Exchange index is right now. Now follow the news for a week. You'll probably notice that the markets don't go up; they soar. They don't go down either, they plunge.

At the end of the week, compare where the TSX is. Chances are, even after all that soaring and plunging, it will be within one or two percent of where it was when we started our little experiment.

So the question is, if it's absolutely routine for the markets to soar and plunge, soar and plunge, soar and plunge, are these really the right words to describe a normal business week?

Absolutely. If you are in the business of getting people's attention, that is. After all, how many people are going to spend a lot of time looking at a story that basically reads "same old stuff going on today, nothing unusual at all."

During this latest bout of volatility some of the stories that I saw in the mainstream press were pretty balanced, actually. Which is cool, since I was expecting more hyperbole. But even balanced reporting can contain some flamboyant language.

I'm reading things like "a rush for the exits", that the markets got "hammered", how they are "in free fall". Even how, from one perspective, July 2007 was worse than what followed the September 11 terrorist activity.

One of the things that I heard was July 25, 2007 was the worst day for the markets since October 19, 1987, a day more commonly known as Black Monday. Whoa, cowboy, time to rein it in a bit.

In a world of soar and plunge, soar and plunge maybe "hammered" isn't out of place, but "worst day since 1987" is over the top. It's a phrase that may technically be accurate, but not from a perspective that anyone really cares about.

On October 19, 1987 the Toronto Stock Exchange 300 Composite Index plunged 407.20 points, (There's that word plunged again!) to close at 3,191.38. On July 25, 2007 the markets plunged 400.17 points. Except this time they closed at 14,068.16.

So why is a 400 point drop in 2007 not as big a deal as a 400 point drop in 1987? Simple math. Taking 400 points off of a 3600 base is a much bigger decline in percent terms than taking 400 points off of a 14,400 base. 400 points in 1987 meant a single day drop of 11.3 percent. In 2007, 400 points is only 2.77 percent.

The bottom line is that these "points" are just a method of measurement. It's the percentage change that counts, and clearly losing 11.3 percent in one day is a bigger deal than losing 2.77 percent. Four times bigger, actually.

Meanwhile, to put the July 2007 headlines in perspective, at the time the Toronto Stock Exchange was up about 13 percent year-to-date. And it's pretty normal for things to cool off when they go up that far that fast.

from August 2007

■ ■ ■ ■ ■ ■

The Alien Battle Cruiser

THIS SUB-PRIME THING sure has some people skittish. Not that sub-prime isn't a valid concern, but I think that many people – Canadians in particular – need to step back and take a fresh look at what's going on, and also at what's not going on.

By "sub-prime" I refer, of course, to the recent practices of American mortgage companies to lend money to people of questionable means to buy real estate at inflated prices. Though perhaps ill-advised, arguably this was feasible when American real estate prices were on the rise and interest rates were low.

This house of cards came crashing down this summer when US real estate prices swooned at the same time that US interest rates started creeping higher. The combination of higher interest costs on loans for depreciated assets means that some of these mortgages are in jeopardy of being defaulted on.

Actually, there is going to be a pretty sizable ripple effect on this one. These shaky mortgages were bundled up and sold as investments. Now the problem is that investors in these types of debt securities don't know how sound their investment is anymore.

But does all this mean that the world is coming to an end? Nah.

It brings to mind a scene from the sci-fi movie, *Men In Black,* with Will Smith and Tommy Lee Jones. Smith is a rookie officer with a top-secret government agency whose mission is to protect life on earth. With the looming destruction of the planet, an excited Smith scolds his partner Jones, "I don't know whether or not you've forgotten, but there's an Alien Battle Cruiser…"

To which the unimpressed veteran Jones replies, "There's always an Alien Battle Cruiser, or Corillean Death Ray, or Intergalactic Plague that's about to wipe out life on this miserable little planet."

From an investment perspective there is always a crisis of confidence, or recession, or inflation, or deflation, or high oil prices, or a trade dispute, or armed hostility that looms larger than life, threatening your hard-earned nest egg.

Of course, through all of these types of events, through wars and recessions and Corillean Death Rays and all the other bad stuff that's happened in the last century, the Dow Jones Industrial Average has gone from 41 points in 1932 to about 13,000 points now. Indeed, the risk was not to be in the markets over those years, but rather to be out of the markets and miss out on all that good, good growth.

But back to sub-prime – is sub-prime really an Alien Battle Cruiser, about to wipe out life on this miserable little planet? Nah.

A little reported fact, in all the huffing and puffing about sub-prime, is that 70 percent of mortgages made in the United States are prime mortgages. Mortgages made to people with good incomes and with solid credit. Mortgages that are not in doubt.

But still there is this prevailing cloud of pessimism, and consequently the shares of many financial service companies have come down in price. Even good companies with minimal exposure to sub-prime concerns.

So what are smart investors doing in this environment? Well, Warren Buffett, the World's Greatest Investor, has been vigorously adding to his positions in financial service companies. I'll come back to Buffett, and what he's doing in a moment.

The fear factor associated with financial businesses has spilled over into Canada, even though most Canadian financial companies are not perceived to be exposed to material sub-prime risk.

Think about this for a moment. Companies that are not exposed to material risk are swept up in the prevailing pessimism of the moment. So is this the time to panic and sell? Quite the opposite, I think.

Now, this is the really important part to note: You need to be selective here. I can't stress this enough. Some stuff has come down in price for good reason.

Just about everyone will have heard the expression "buy low". But simply buying low says nothing of quality.

In other words, let's say a product sells a little more cheaply now than it did before, but at the end of the day the product is really just junk. Just because it sells cheaply doesn't mean that you want to buy it. Sure it's cheap, but that just makes it cheap junk, and that's probably not an attractive thing to be adding to your investment portfolio.

But what if something is diamond-grade, and it sells for less than it used to? Is that something that a person might want to consider purchasing? Absolutely! And that's the stuff that Buffett is buying – wonderful companies with minimal risk whose shares have been beaten up in this swell of pessimism. Not cheap junk, but diamond-grade companies that are selling at wonderfully attractive prices.

Earlier I mentioned that Canadians in particular should perhaps step back and take a second look at the current market environment; about what is going on, and also what's not going on. Tune out all that noise that's being made about sub-prime or Intergalactic Plagues or whatever the latest fear factor is, and take a rational, unemotional look. Because there's always an Alien Battle Cruiser approaching, and yet the Dow still went from 41 to 13,000.

Different people are going to do different things in this environment, and they are going to have different results. I already told you what Buffett is doing.

What are you going to do?

from November 2007

■ ■ ■ ■ ■ ■

Interesting, But Is It News?

THE DAY THAT I sat down to write this essay had a bit of a theme to it. The news of the day.

My day started with a client dropping off a copy of a story from the National Post that he wanted me to see. This was another of those stories suggesting that the global economy was circling the drain, and chaos was inevitable.

It was an interesting article, but let's be clear here. It's not news.

What it is, is one gentleman's opinion of what might happen. That's all. Now, I'm not suggesting that the author's opinion isn't valid. I'm not suggesting that at all. I'm just stating the obvious in that there is a night and day difference between opinion and fact.

Here's a little analogy. I'm a hockey fan, and in a few weeks the NHL playoffs will start. 16 teams will make the playoffs, and I'd expect that each and every one of those 16 teams has at least a handful of supporters fanatical enough to think that their team is going to win.

So we've got at least 16 different opinions, some of which will be loudly made and persuasively argued, on who is going to win the Stanley Cup. But only one of them will be right.

The next time the news came up was later in the day when another client asked me how much I watched the business channel on TV. "Never," I replied. Which, I suppose isn't technically true. I have seen it in the past, just not in recent memory.

In fact, we just got a new satellite TV subscription, and over the last few days I've been playing around with it, trying to figure out how it works. And during this time it never even crossed my mind to find CNBC.

Something else happened today though. Something that made me want to check out the news. Not just read the news of the day, but to actively seek information on a news story. It's March 10, and today's the day that the allegations about New York Governor and former Attorney General Eliot Spitzer's involvement in a prostitution scandal were made public.

I'm trying to think of how often that I would be curious to know the details of sex scandal allegations on an American politician. Only two positions come to mind; the President of the United States and the Chair of the US Federal Reserve.

So why would I care whether the Governor of New York got caught with a high-priced call girl? It's because Spitzer is very well known in the investment world.

As New York Attorney General, Spitzer trumpeted about like an avenging angel, cleaning up questionable practices and dodgy accounting, and prosecuting white collar crooks. Spitzer took to his job with zeal, earning the nickname "The Sheriff of Wall Street." He was even touted as a potential presidential candidate.

Although the types of problems that Spitzer was looking to address were not common practice in Canada, Spitzer did have an indirect impact in his role as top cop in the biggest securities market in the world.

Even though none of the allegations against Spitzer have been proven, just being implicated may be enough to finish his career as a politician. In the meantime, Spitzer's critics are all over the hypocrisy of a man that used to prosecute prostitution rings being a client himself, assuming that the allegations are true.

I ended up getting home late on this day, and the family is already tucked into bed, so as I'm having a late supper I tune into CNN to see what's being said. I ended up watching TV for a few hours. First CNN, then the Business News Network, then CNBC.

What I saw was a few minutes of actual news (the allegations against Spitzer), then a few hours of people talking about it. It was entertaining, but the news took minutes and the opinions took hours.

One of the commentators made an interesting point. He said that only in the US would this be front-page news. I think that there is a lot of truth to that.

In a society that gave us The Jerry Springer Show and the televised trial of O.J. Simpson, people want entertainment. And what could be more entertaining that the tawdry details of a spectacular fall from grace?

My point is that this is not news. The pundits were discussing what could happen next, not what has actually happened. And discuss it they did. For hours.

It makes for good television, though. It's entertaining. People tune in. Ratings go up. Advertising revenues go up. And that's why there was endless coverage of Spitzer, but no mention of the suicide bombings in Pakistan that killed 24 people.

So there is news, and then there are opinions. There are facts, and then there is speculation. There is information, and then there is entertainment. A person would be well served not to allow these distinctions to become blurred.

At the end of my night I flicked over to the Business News Network one last time. They were running paid TV programming. How ironically appropriate.

From March 2008

What Does Psychic Nikki Say?

THIS IS THE TIME of the year that some financial pundits are going to try to tell you what to expect investments to do in 2008. I'm not one of those people though.

I'm not much for short-term predictions. In my mind there is just one surefire way to tell you what happens in 2008, and that is to write about it in January 2009.

For what it's worth, though, the general consensus seems to be that in 2008 the Canadian dollar will remain somewhere around par, the U.S. economy will slow down further, and the markets will be just as volatile as they were this summer.

All that sounds reasonable enough, I guess. I mean, I'm not going to disagree with it. But that doesn't mean that I necessarily agree with these predictions either. Frankly, my crystal ball is a little cloudy, and I really can't tell you what is going to happen tomorrow.

However, as I was researching this essay I did find someone who apparently can predict the future. Her name is Psychic Nikki.

Unfortunately, it appears that even Psychic Nikki isn't perfect on her timing. Her 2006 predictions didn't pan out, so she carried them over to 2007. And while these same forecasts didn't come to pass in 2007 either, Psychic Nikki feels quite strongly that 2008 is finally the year that her predictions will come true. For really real, this time. 2008 is definitely the year.

As they say in the clairvoyant game, if you are going to forecast the future, do it often. Sooner or later you'll get it right. And that's when you can tell all your friends that they should have listened.

Seriously though, one year ago how many people were predicting that in 2007 we would see a collapse of the US housing market, a global credit crunch, oil at $100 USD per barrel, gold at $850 USD per ounce, and the loonie on par with the US greenback? Some people did, sure. But they were in the minority.

A year ago the consensus was that stock markets were in for a bull year, and commodities like oil and gold were probably due for a breather. Oops. So why did so many "experts" get things wrong?

Well, the reality is that human beings simply do not have the ability to know the future. It doesn't matter how smart you are, how experienced you are, or how good your computer algorithms are. Sorry 'bout that, Psychic Nikki.

Now we can come up with really good guesses sometimes, and often that's enough to swing the odds in our favour. But nobody, not even Warren Buffett, knows precisely what the future will bring. Years ago, when someone asked him a question about where interest rates were going, he said, "Only two people understand that. Both of them live in Switzerland. However, they're diametrically opposed to each other."

So given that nobody, not even Buffett, knows with certainty what the future will bring, what's an investor to do?

The answer is simple. Diversify.

Proper diversification means that you can face an uncertain future with some degree of confidence that things are going to turn out all right.

Unfortunately, most people are not as diversified as they think. In the summer a lady asked me for an opinion on her portfolio. She had 15 different mutual funds from multiple companies, so she figured that she had lots of eggs in lots of baskets. She was wrong.

What she really had was the same ideas over and over again. Of particular concern were two products that, as it was explained to her, would serve her well in times of changing interest rates. If interest rates went up then one product was supposed to do well. If interest rates went down, then the other was supposed to prosper.

In reality though, and despite what she was told by her mutual fund salesperson, these two products were not at all different. Far from it, in fact, as they were actually 97 percent the same. She had more than one mutual fund, but she had no diversification.

If you aren't diversified then these market predictions become much more important. If you are overly concentrated in interest-sensitive investments then, all of a sudden, it becomes much more important to get a handle on the direction of interest rates.

The only problem with that is that the two guys who know where interest rates are going live in Switzerland. And they don't agree with each other. So which one of them are you going to listen to?

Rather than trying to know the unknowable, I say just diversify. Then relax. Relax because proper diversification means that you can face uncertain times, and come through all right. Regardless of what Psychic Nikki says.

From January 2008

■ ■ ■ ■ ■ ■

Of Our Troubles, No Man Can See the End

THERE IS CERTAINLY no shortage of gloomy economic headlines these days. The newspapers are full of dire predictions of impending doom. Here's one of my favourites:

"It is a gloomy moment in the history of our country… The domestic economic situation is in chaos. Our dollar is weak throughout the world… It is a solemn moment. Of our troubles, no man can see the end."

Wow. That is pretty solemn. "Of our troubles, no man can see the end." Not much room for optimism there.

But this type of grim sentiment appears to be omnipresent at the moment. So what's so special about this one quotation? I mean, why would I single out these remarks in particular as being worthy of special attention?

Well, what makes this particular quotation stand out is its vintage. These words appeared in Harper's Weekly in 1857.

Obviously, despite the author's pessimism, the world did not end in 1857. And, just as obviously, the propagation of gloomy headlines has not abated in the time from then 'til now.

Here's a more recent headline in December from The Seattle Times that was brought to my attention; "Experts: Bank Crisis Risks Turning Recession Into Depression." The story talks about the credit crunch, and says "… the banking crisis is no joke. It is real – so real it risks turning the emerging recession into the biggest economic nightmare since the Great Depression of the 1930s." One guy is on record as saying "My own view of this tends to be apocalyptic."

Okay, that kind of prognostication really is no joke. The thing about it is, the word "depression" gets bandied about so often nowadays we've become numbed to what a depression really entails. During the Great Depression in the 1930s we had a 20 percent unemployment rate. That means one person in five is out of work. The US Gross Domestic Product was chopped in half. Try to imagine what things would be like if half of the economy went away.

With the Great Depression we had severe and terrible and prolonged disruptions, both social and economic. A second Great Depression would literally be the end of the world as we know it, for a while anyway. We've seen a lot of economic unpleasantness in the last 90 years, but we have never had anything that has even come close to rivalling the Great Depression.

In fact, virtually all comparisons to the Great Depression are just plain silly. Unemployment today is roughly 6.5 percent, not 20 percent. Today we are looking at a far more modest economic slowdown; a small fraction of the 50 percent decline that happened in the 1930s.

This indiscriminate use of extreme words, such as "apocalyptic", is not limited to economic stories. Sometimes coming up on the wrong end of a sports scoreboard is described a tragic loss. That's silly. A tragedy is the recent terrorist attacks in India. Losing a hockey game is not a tragedy.

Okay, so here's the thing about this projected economic "apocalypse": This story ran in The Seattle Times in December, but it was December, 1990. And, obviously we didn't have a depression in the 1990s. A recession, yes. But a full-out depression? We didn't come even remotely close.

Right now there is a lot of fear, and there is a lot of pessimism. There are "expert" predictions of imminent disaster. That's nothing new. For at least 150 years people have thought that of our troubles, no man can see the end. This was true in the 1850s. This was true in the 1930s. This was even true in the 1990s.

Coinciding with pessimism, there are phenomenal investment opportunities available right now. In fact, right now we are having a Big Bear Sale. We have this sale every 5 or 6 years or so. It always coincides with the prevailing sentiment that of our troubles, no man can see the end.

I can't tell you how long the Big Bear Sale will last. Chances are the sale will end without advance notice. But I can tell you that your long-term investment results are largely determined by how much money you put to work right now, before the Big Bear Sale inevitably ends.

As the great Warren Buffett says, "The time to be fearful is when others are greedy, and the time to be greedy is when others are fearful."

From December 2008

■ ■ ■ ■ ■ ■

The Problem with Predictions

YEARS AGO I wrote an essay about the provocative Harry Dent, a well-known prognosticator who bases his predictions on demographics. Demography is the study of human populations, and it can be a useful forecasting tool on a macro scale.

In a nutshell, as a person moves through different stages of life they tend to have similar wants and needs. What is important to someone in their twenties will not be the same things that are important to someone in their seventies. The twenty-something person is thinking about buying stuff like sports equipment, houses, cars, and education. The seventy-something person is thinking about buying stuff like financial services, and health care, and leisure.

Knowing how many twenty-something people are out there, and how many seventy-something people, are out there means we can predict things. Things like the demand for specific goods and services, the need for health care, and the need for education.

So how does all of this fit into making stock market predictions? Well, basically the premise is that the baby-boomers would drive the stock market up and up until they began to retire, at which time the stock market was in for a very rough time. Hard times were forecasted to continue until the next big population wave begins to spend and invest.

Okay, all that sounds reasonable. The only problem is that the predictions for market performance based purely on demographics have been disastrously inaccurate.

When I first wrote about Dent he was predicting the Dow Jones Industrial Average would hit 41,000 by 2008. Well, here it is a year past the target date, and the Dow is sitting at less than one quarter of where it should be according to that bold, but perhaps feckless, prediction.

Why we are again talking about Mr. Dent is because I just ran across one of his books. I was at the local library and it was in the discard bin, so I snagged it.

This book was written in 2006, and the subtitle of this work is "How to profit from the Greatest Boom in History: 2006 – 2010." In the book Dent is still predicting the Dow will hit 40,000. He's just extended the time frame a bit to mid- to late 2010.

That breathtaking prediction, full of hope and promise, struck a chord with people. Dent is a New York Times bestselling author. Popularity and accuracy are two different things, however. Now that 2010 is just a few short months away I think you would be hard pressed to find anyone at all that would call the last four years "the Greatest Boom in History."

Every thorn has its rose though, and Mr. Dent does occasionally discuss some useful things. But as for "how to profit from the Greatest Boom in History: 2006 – 2010," forget it. The accuracy of these forecasts are worthless. Worse than worthless, maybe, as anyone who depended on them would have been severely punished.

As a cautionary tale, however, this is priceless. You see, these types of stock market predictions are market-timing on the grandest scale. And now we are getting to the point of all this – market timing simply does not work. I can't do it. You can't do it. Dent can't do it. End of story.

I agree with Dent that the Dow will inevitably be at 41,000. I've got no doubt about that. Using historical rates of return, and doing the calculation in my head, I'd say it will happen in another 15 years or so.

Please keep in mind that I took all of about 10 seconds to work this out. I can't tell you with pinpoint precision exactly when the Dow will hit 41,000. Clearly, though, neither can Dent. Or anyone else, for that matter.

Here's an analogy. Let's say that my job is to predict when the sun will set tomorrow. So I say, and with great conviction of course, that it will happen at 12:00 noon. But when tomorrow comes, and the sun doesn't set at noon, I update my prediction to 12:01 p.m. And then when that also doesn't transpire, I amend my prediction to 12:02 p.m.

Finally, after a few hundred wrong guesses, I eventually get it right. And then that's when I get to say, "See I told you so, I can predict when the sun will set."

Well, okay, maybe in my analogy I finally do get things right, but realistically, where is the utility in that? If I am inaccurate to the tune of 15 years, how useful is my fortune telling? Even a stopped clock is right twice a day, but that doesn't mean that you can depend on a stopped clock to tell you the time.

The basic problem with market timing is that the galaxy does not know that you are doing it. Just when you think you've got things all figured out, the butterfly on the other side of the planet flaps his wings, and even if you get your predictions mostly right you can still be quite wrong.

The economy, the tech crash, the accounting scandals, the terrorists, and the natural disasters all must have missed Dent's original memo about unfettered growth from 2000 to 2008. The economy, the U.S. real estate bubble, sub-prime loans, asset-backed commercial paper, and the policy makers who changed the taxation of income trusts all must have missed Dent's 2006 book, and the promise of the Greatest Boom in History from 2006 to 2010.

There are things that work, and there are things that don't. Market timing is folly. It falls squarely into the category of things that don't work, regardless of how many books it sells.

From October 2009

Financial News as Entertainment

FREQUENT READERS OF these essays will probably have noted that I have much disdain for the tabloid circus that masquerades as informed, timely and valuable wisdom on matters of finance. In fact, I'm often bitterly disappointed about the lack of knowledge demonstrated by supposedly knowledgeable people.

Don't get me wrong, I'm not saying that Joe the Plumber needs night courses in economics. But I do think that people that hold themselves out as having some kind of financial authority should have at least a working knowledge of the subject matter. I don't think that's too much to ask.

Anyways, just for fun, I recently recorded half a day of broadcasting from one of those business news channels. Now, in this case, I am fully expecting these people to know their subject matter. But what I am looking for this time is a little different.

I expect these people to know what they are talking about. I just want to see if anybody should care about what they're saying.

See, here's the thing — there was nothing at all special about the day I picked to record half a day of programming. The thought occurred to me to do this for the purposes of this essay, and so I recorded the broadcasting on a Monday in April. Nothing more, nothing less.

The day in question was April 18, 2011. There was no federal budget that day. No extraordinary economic or human catastrophe to report on. In fact, really nothing of note happened on this particular Monday. It was a day like any other.

The biggest business story of the day was that one of the bond rating agencies warned the US government that their credit rating could suffer if they kept spending money. Which isn't much of a story when you think of it. Please note, the story isn't that the US credit rating has changed – it hasn't, the USA still has a triple A rating – just that if the US keeps spending money that credit rating might be reduced. Kinda underwhelming as news stories go, but whaddya going to do on a slow news day?

North American markets happened to close down that day, but it was just a normal day of trading. The markets recovered the next day and, since I am getting around to writing this essay a week after I recorded these programs, I can tell you that the markets finished the week nicely positive. April 18, 2011 really was just a normal, nondescript day.

And that's the worst day possible for a 24-hour business news channel.

How are you going to get Joe the Plumber to tune in if the biggest story of the day is that if the US keeps spending money their credit rating may suffer? On its own, that's not a particularly sexy story. In fact, it's not really a story at all. It's a scenario that might happen. Or it might not. And in either case Joe isn't really going to need a lot of expert commentary to figure out the nuances of how spending too much money can affect a credit rating.

So, if you have a 24-hour business news channel, what are you going to talk about round the clock if nothing noteworthy is happening? We're about to find out.

My thesis, which isn't really a thesis but rather more of a truism, is that 24-hour business news channels aren't in the education and information business at all. They are in the entertainment business. And if you are in the entertainment business you can always find something to fill the airtime, even on a slow news day.

My experiment will be to see how much of the programming is educational and how much is entertainment. The expected outcome of this experiment is that 95 percent of what passes for financial journalism will be focused on what to expect over the next couple of months. But that's not educational, it's entertainment, and a low form of entertainment at that.

That's because people start talking about variables that no one can either predict or control, and further these are variables that almost always end up surprising the people making the predictions. And if that wasn't enough, in the big picture, this isn't the stuff that matters anyway. Whether you achieve your financial objectives or not has pretty much no correlation whatsoever to whether Caterpillar shares fell 3 percent on April 18, 2011 after gaining 51 percent over the last year.

It's a cacophony of noise about meaningless, minute trivia. It's the silliest form of commentary imaginable, and it fills 24 hours of broadcasting each day.

Far more useful would be a discussion on how to design a portfolio that would produce sustainable income over a 30 year retirement in a rising cost world. Or the factors that go into a decision about whether to pay off your mortgage, or use that money elsewhere. Or how to take full advantage of the Registered Education Savings Plan.

These are conversations that matter. But that's not what I expect that I'm about to see.

So, with all that being said, I'm pressing play and here we go...

And, it took all of a few seconds for my expectations to be validated. The very first program looks at what happened in the last hour of trading. Seriously, that's the description of the program. Analyzing the markets based on the last hour of trading on Wall Street. As if that has any kind of significance. It makes about as much sense as dissecting two minutes of the second period of an NHL hockey game played in November to try to determine who is going to win the Stanley Cup.

With passion and a lot of arm waving, the importance of minute and meaningless data is inflated to having ground-shaking potential. Listening to these guys you'd think the sky was falling. But with the benefit of hindsight I already know that the week was positive. The terrible pronouncements of Monday afternoon were quickly forgotten by Tuesday morning.

Let's see if the rest of the programming is any better. More on the credit rating non-story. About seven hours more as a matter of fact. The fast forward button saw frequent use.

But then, surprise! Something useful, and from the least likely of sources. The guy with most flamboyant personality of all – a guy that previously I had never heard say anything other than financial smut – starts his program saying "you need to have conviction. You have to believe in something and have the confidence to stick with those beliefs even when the market doesn't always go your way in the short term." That, my friends, is absolutely true.

In the end, it looks like the 95 percent rule – that financial journalism is 95 percent entertainment and 5 percent useful information – seems to hold true. Here's how you can test the theory.

One year from now take a look back at the stories that currently are being positioned as the driving forces, and see how many have staying power. Some stories of today will still be topical, sure.

But for some context, a year ago people were saying that the government bailout of General Motors was going to be a colossal, mind-numbing, money-burning flop that jeopardized our very standard of living. Instead it turned out to be a resounding success.

Just something to keep in mind the next time that the financial media says the world is ending yet again, or assigns some special significance to whether Governor of the Bank of Canada Mark Carney had coffee or tea with lunch.

From April 2011

■ ■ ■ ■ ■ ■

The 95 Percent Rule

IT'S SUNDAY EVENING, and I'm doing my reading, as I am wont to do. The theme for the day's reading: as it so often is – bad news.

Bad news. Bad news. Bad news.

Terrible forecasts of continued economic misery. Hopelessness and despair at every turn. Doom and gloom, ad infinitum.

I read about "an American economy deteriorating before our eyes." I read about how "government stimuli are worsening the structural imbalances underlying our economy." I read about "massive Wealth Destruction." (So, why the capital letters? Is 'Wealth Destruction' now a recognized fixture, akin to the World Series?) I read about how "Two bear markets and a housing market collapse have put the American consumer on the ropes. And the next bear market will bring him to the canvas."

Blah, blah, blah.

The stuff I am reading is relentless. Every article pounding home the same message. Over and over.

Even when the message is clearly exaggerated.

I read a piece from Time Magazine about the legal appeal of the charges against the convicted former CEO of Enron. Since I am reading the online version I can quickly link to other stories. And Time Magazine has no shortage of suggestions.

Sprinkled through the story (in bold font and red letters, of course) I can link to pictures of the top 10 scared stock traders. Then a list of the top 10 crooked CEOs. Then the 25 people to blame for the financial crisis. Then the top 10 financial collapses. Then the top 10 worst business deals. All of this in a 596-word story on a guy that was convicted three years ago.

Apparently the format of the article was to write a paragraph, insert a link to a semi-related top 10 nasty things list. Write another paragraph, insert another list. And just keep repeating until you either run out of story or you run out of lists.

Out of curiosity, I clicked on the link to see the pictures of the top 10 scared stockbrokers. I mean, how does a person make it onto that list? Is it a timed event, or is there some kind of head-to-head showdown, or what? Is there a regional playoff to determine who advances to the national stage? Just how does one determine which stockbroker is the scaredest, anyway?

As it turns out the link just has pictures of people who apparently are supposed to be stockbrokers. It's probably best that Time Magazine didn't clutter the photo-essay with the distinction between what a stockbroker does and what happens on the stock exchange floor. It's just easier to call everyone a stockbroker.

Be that as it may, these pictures are fantastic. It's clear that these pictures were taken by a professional. These guys and gals look like they were just told that they have leukemia. The facial expressions are of panic and rage and desperation and grief and anguish and grim determination, and it is all beautifully captured by the camera lens.

I start reading the captions, and I notice that a few of the photos were taken in October. I actually said out loud (in a puzzled voice, no less), "What? Are they talking about this year?"

It was just a reaction. I was alone and wasn't talking to anyone, but I was confused. Stock market activity in October 2009 was fine. It was normal. No colossal set-backs to speak of. Nothing to merit the "top 10 scaredest stockbrokers" anyway. The photo-essay refers to the Dow Jones Industrial Average a lot, but the Dow Jones finished the month of October fractionally ahead of where it started.

I'm not connecting the dots on this yet, so I go through the pictures again. This time looking not just at the dates, but also at what has gotten these "stockbrokers" so despondent that they make the "most scared" list.

One of the pictures was from a day when the Dow Jones Industrial Average dropped 124 points. Okay, let me give you some context on that. That's about as newsworthy as northern Canada seeing -20 Celsius temperatures in the middle of winter. It happens fairly routinely.

So, although the event itself is nothing special, the picture is great. Boom! All of a sudden this guy finds himself on a list of scared stockbrokers.

Who knows what the guys in the pictures are actually reacting to? Maybe their kid failed her math exam. Maybe their cat just died. Maybe they have a wicked hangover.

It made me think of the lyrics from the Tragically Hip song, 'Yawning or Snarling:'

Take a look at this photograph
Clearly his teeth were bared
He could have been yawning or snarling
The story was never clear

Great pictures though. They are worth a thousand words. The only question is, which words?

Which brings me to one of the other things that I read on that Sunday night. The 95 Percent Rule.

The 95 Percent Rule is remarkably straightforward. It says that 95 percent of what you read about economics and finance is either wrong or irrelevant.

Sounds about right to me.

From November 2009

Disasters Don't Arrive by Appointment

So I am sitting down to write this essay, and it's July 29, 2011. The timing of the writing is important.

You see, lately I have had the occasional person ask me what I think of this most recent episode in the Never-Ending Doomsday Chronicles, midsummer 2011 edition. (For convenience, the Never-Ending Doomsday Chronicles are hereafter referred to by the acronym NEDC.)

These are not just questions from laypeople, either. I've also had a number of advisors ask me about this, as they are fielding similar NEDC questions from their own clients.

I guess my response might be characterized as patriarchal amusement.

That's a response that they probably weren't expecting, and, to be honest, it doesn't really go over all that well. But I just can't help it. It's hard to get worked up about the latest episode when some new version of Financial Armageddon comes along every couple of weeks, the latest epic chapter in the NEDC.

Chagrined, the fearful herd will have pointed, follow-up inquiries. Am I not taking this seriously? Do I not understand the consequences of the US defaulting on their obligations? Who the hell am I to disagree with the Talking Heads on TV? Or their brother's buddy's neighbor, who is a really, smart guy who has done very well for himself, and he knows for sure that the world is ending; for really, real this time?

What am I supposed to say to that? Sure, I am taking it seriously. Well, seriously enough to understand the issue, that is. But just because I understand the issue doesn't mean that I agree with Chicken Little. Sorry, but I am not about to validate your paranoia by playing the NEDC game.

In case anyone missed what all the hullabaloo is about, the USA is supposed to run out of cash in about 3 days from the time of this writing. After that, unless something is done, ostensibly the Americans will not be in a position to fulfill all their obligations.

The potential consequences of inaction would be widespread uncertainty, a likely downgrade of the US credit rating, increased borrowing costs, and, more or less, general anarchy. There are different perspectives on what to do about this; the Democrats think that the answer to the problem is to authorize more borrowings, while the Republicans think that they should spend less.

Note the critical part of the above description, *"unless something is done"*. And I can assure you that something will be done. So much so that I am willing to go right out on a limb, and tell you in advance that an answer will be revealed sometime between now as I write this, and next week when you read it.

You see, disasters don't arrive by appointment. The US debt ceiling is the worst kept secret in the world. Do you really think they won't find a fix?

It would be like if you and your buddy were in a car, and you were driving straight towards the Grand Canyon. You are only 200 kilometers away from hurtling to your certain deaths, and you are travelling at 100 kmh. In just 2 hours you are going to drive right off the precipice and, if that happens, you will die. You've got 2 hours to make a decision, and you have some options. Maybe you want to turn left in order to avoid disaster, but your buddy thinks turning right is the better option. So you argue about it for almost 2 hours. But at the end someone is going to make a decision, because the consequences of not making a decision are worse than not getting your way.

Straight up, I don't care what chapter of the Never-Ending Doomsday Chronicles the Talking Heads are reading from. Folks, this is not Financial Armageddon.

Speaking about the Talking Heads reading from the NEDC, there is a brilliant exchange between a Talking Head and a US Congressman that went viral. The Talking Head is trying to emphasize that this chapter of the NEDC is just really nasty (as are all chapters of the NEDC), but the Congressman is just not playing.

The Talking Head, who I guess is qualified to discuss matters of economic policy because she has a degree in *Broadcast Journalism*, asks the Congressman, in an increasingly frantic pitch…

"You are simplifying the issues that were on the plate of the nation at the time. We were looking at reverting to a Depression at that point. Everyone, the Fed Chairman…"

At that point the Congressman, having heard enough of raving, politely intervened. "Well, I disagree that we were going into a Depression."

The Talking Head sputters, obviously upset that her tirade was interrupted, "Do you have a degree in Economics?"

The Congressman replies, "Yes, Ma'am, I do. Highest honors."

Economists 1. Broadcast Journalists 0. Folks, this is not Financial Armageddon. Disasters don't arrive by appointment

The Never Ending Doomsday Chronicles is pretty much just a comic book; heroic struggles with evil villains, and peril at every turn. And, whatever happens, there is a brand new edition on the newsstands next week.

From July 2011

■ ■ ■ ■ ■ ■

Déjà Vu All Over Again

A FEW OF MY RECENT ESSAYS have referred to the situation in Greece. The quick summary is A) Greece is not the problem that some in the media portray it, and B) the correct action is not to flee but to take advantage of the opportunity.

These essays have drawn some response; particularly from one of my colleagues, who I believe is of the opinion that A) Greece might be the tip of the iceberg, and B) maybe fleeing might not be that bad an idea after all.

The reality of writing a thousand or so words each week is that it can be hard to get into deep detail on complex issues, and Greece is a complex issue. So allow me to elaborate now.

I'm not saying that there aren't any problems in Greece. In fact, in the original essay which ran last month, I said that Greece would probably default on its debt. The point wasn't that Greece didn't have problems but rather, with Greece's miniscule economy and extensive history of past default, why would anyone care?

What I was getting at was the size of the problem, and the attention that the problem is getting, is not in proportion. And that's the way it is now that we have 24-hour news channels fuelled by 17 hours of live programming each and every day. Every potential news story is examined for all possible dramatic angles. Few of these types of stories live up to their hype.

Right now I'm looking at a small story that ran this summer that says fish in British Columbia are safe to eat. Why is that a story? Well, you may recall the significant fuss that was made about food safety in the days following the earthquake in Japan.

If you don't recall the fuss, I'll remind you. After the disaster at the Fukushima nuclear power plant, people were worried about whether their food was fit for human consumption given the potential for radiation exposure. Spinach in particular was identified as potentially dangerous. The coverage went on for weeks.

Why is this? Simple. Radioactive food scares people. Global economic meltdowns scare people. And scared people will tune in for the buzz on what might happen next.

My dissenting colleague states that the problems may spill over into other European countries. I don't disagree; that may indeed happen. In fact, although it's not stated in the article, that's the kind of thing that I was thinking of when I wrote in the original piece that there are bigger things to worry about than Greece. Greece is one thing, contagion is another.

But I didn't go into detail in the original piece on some kind of domino theory along the lines of the "For Want of a Nail" nursery rhyme. You remember that one...

> For want of a nail the shoe was lost. For want of a shoe the horse was lost. For want of horse the rider was lost. For want of a rider the battle was lost. For want of a battle the kingdom was lost. And all for the want of a horseshoe nail.

So a person could say that Greece tips over Italy, which sinks the European Union, which abandons the United States, which drowns the world. You could say that. Some people are.

BUT NOT EVERYONE. Here's a quote that I recently came across.

> I think the future of equities will be roughly the same as their past; in particular, common-stock purchases will prove satisfactory when made at appropriated price levels. It may be objected that it is far too cursory and superficial a conclusion; that it fails to take into account the new factors and problems that have entered the economic picture in recent years – especially those of ... the movement towards less consumption and zero growth. Perhaps I should add to my list the widespread public mistrust of Wall Street as a whole, engendered by its well-nigh scandalous behavior during recent years in the areas of ethics, financial practices of all sorts, and plain business sense."

To really understand this quote, you need to know who said it, and more importantly, when it was said. While it sounds like it came from last week's news, this quote is from Ben Graham, the father of value investing and mentor of Warren Buffett. He said that in 1974, and at the time the S&P 500 was down 48 percent.

So when we look at the problems of today – of Grecian debt, of radioactive spinach – are these problems worse than the problems of the 1970s? A time when we had OPEC causing energy prices to triple? When we had economic conditions so terrible that economists had to coin a brand new term – stagflation – to describe the simultaneous occurrence of crippling unemployment and devastating inflation, conditions formerly thought of as being mutually exclusive?

By the way, a year after the Graham article the S&P 500 was up 37 percent. Despite the issues of the day the world did not come to a screeching halt then. I don't think it's about to now. This time is not different.

But – and this is important – if it's not Greece that is a problem, it could just as easily be something else, and probably it's something that isn't even anticipated yet.

So here's what you need to know. First, growing your money involves different strategies than protecting your money. And second, when I talk about investing I always mean investing for the long-term.

If you have a short-term time frame, take the reliable road. Don't be in equities, with their daily fluctuations. Be in something like a high daily interest savings account, where you can depend on your money being there for you when you need it.

"Investing" with a short time frame, perhaps thinking that the Greece situation will quickly resolve itself, is not investing. It's speculation. A notable securities firm in the US just went bankrupt speculating on the EU debt situation.

Speculation is a completely different conversation than investing. It's a conversation that I rarely have because I'm not a speculator. If you want to speculate, go nuts, but I have no insight into what will happen in the next 3 or 4 months.

What I'm saying is that I fully expect things to be up over the next 3 or 4 years. So take the long-term perspective and accept that there will be bumps along the way. I can't tell you when the bumps will happen, or what the cause is, but I can assure you that they will occur. It's the cost of admission. In order to be there for the good days you have to be ready for the bad days.

This is the part to understand – for the true long-term investor, the bumps are not the most important thing. Let's say you are 20 years away from retirement, and when retirement does happen you are going to stretch your nest egg out over 25 years. The important thing isn't what happened in the fourth week of November 2011, but rather are you going to have enough money to do the things that you want to do over a multi-decade retirement in a rising cost world?

And don't forget – despite Grecian debt and radioactive spinach – this time is not different. It never is.

From November 2011

PART TWO

Why Do Smart People Do Dumb Things?

The fear of missing out is a powerful thing.

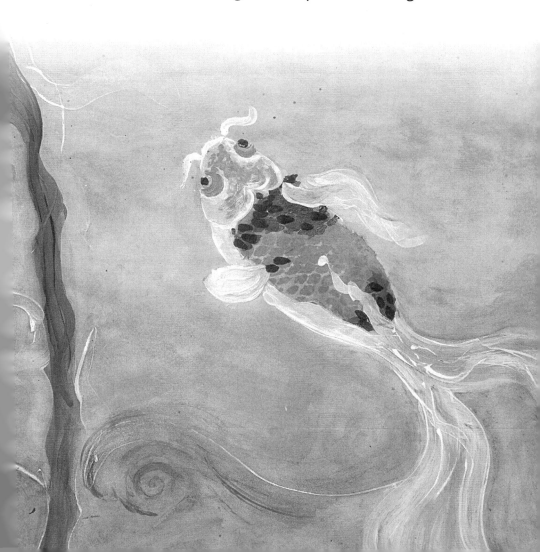

■ ■ ▪ ▪ ▪ ▪

Don't Believe Everything You Read

EVERYONE IS ENTITLED to have an opinion. But there is a world of difference between opinion and truth. An opinion is a personal judgment on the state of things. The truth is the real state of things.

One of the things that I became very aware of when I began writing is that some people actually believe what they see in print to be the truth. And lots of times it is the truth. If you read in the paper that the Vancouver Canucks won last night's hockey game then you can be pretty safe in the assumption that the Vancouver Canucks really did win last night's hockey game.

On the other hand, a lot of stuff that gets published is just someone's opinion. Books, magazines, even this essay – many of these things are published opinions, and the fact that somebody went to the effort of getting the material published often lends validity to the opinion.

And that's a good thing. Learning more about what other people think is valuable. Even if you disagree with an opinion, oftentimes it is still worthwhile to hear someone out. But the critical part that makes this worthwhile, and this really is the crux of the matter, is that what they have to say, even if you disagree with it, is valid to start with.

You see, sometimes really, really bad advice from unqualified sources gets published. Even, I recently discovered, in otherwise-reputable national financial planning magazines.

It really came to my attention that an article was published in a Canadian financial planning magazine claiming that mortgage insurance was far superior to life insurance. Now, mortgage insurance is fine for what it does, but the thing about this whole boondoggle was the "expert" who wrote the piece is a self-confessed amateur, with no insurance training, who draws conclusions out of thin air based on erroneous information and, for unknown reasons, has a bone to pick with the insurance industry.

He carefully concocted a scenario that presents mortgage insurance in the best possible light, ignoring many very salient points. It's a biased piece, based on conclusions that he made up himself back in the 1980's.

And yet the article was published as "expert opinion." Now the important point here is that this is not a merely a difference of opinion. It's not like we are debating term vs. permanent insurance, and while we may disagree, both sides have valid points.

Rather the article in question has been proven to be false, deceptive, malicious, and dangerous. And that's not just my opinion. The opposition to the piece was unanimous. When asked to defend his position the author's arguments could not stand up to the slightest bit of scrutiny. The work published as "expert opinion" was really just the out-of-date rantings of a rude, bitter, sad, confused and very mistaken person.

And yet, it was published as "expert opinion." Now, if he was writing that he has perfected a methodology to grow dandelions in winter, or something that is relatively benign, then nobody really needs to care about what he says, because it's pretty much harmless.

But he's not talking about dandelions, he's talking about insurance, and that is deadly serious stuff. It's what protects your family. You don't trifle with stuff that protects your family.

Here's an analogy. Let's say I am a self-declared expert on fires. I mean I claim to know fires inside and out. Campfires, bonfires, barbeques, wood stoves, all of it. In fact, I have even written a book, entitled "The Canadian Guide to Fires: Everything you need to know."

Now I haven't actually worked in any field that directly relates to fires, and I have no formal training in fires, but I did go to university 30 years ago, where I studied several things, including wood. For instance, I know that wood comes from trees.

And since we also know that wood is combustible, and I studied wood 30 years ago, I certainly feel that I am more than qualified to declare myself an expert on fires, and to write a book about fires. In fact, it is clear to me that, since I studied wood 30 years ago, I know even more about fires than the people with up-to-date training and experience in actual fires.

So, in my expert opinion, the best way to start a fire is to use lots of gasoline and then throw a match on it. It doesn't even matter what kind of fire it is, always use lots and lots of gas. You see, gas burns real good. So when you are having a backyard BBQ, or heating your house with wood heat, be sure to use lots of gasoline. You can trust me on this. I wrote a book.

Okay, back to reality. We all know that using lots and lots of gasoline then throwing a match to start a fire certainly can get a fire going, but it's not the only way to light a fire. In fact, not only is this fire-starting method dangerous, but there are alternative fire-starting products that are better, and using gas can be expensive. Sometimes starting a fire with gas actually might be the best way, but often it will not be a good way at all.

It's the same with mortgage insurance. It can work, but much like always starting a fire with gasoline, there is more often than not a better way. Also, similar to my gasoline analogy, mortgage insurance can be dangerous, inferior, and expensive. The danger comes from mortgage insurance being underwritten at time of claim, not at time of issue, and mortgage insurance is not portable. The inferiority of mortgage insurance comes from the ownership of the policy, the beneficiary options, and the length and amount of coverage. The potentially expensive nature of mortgage insurance is because of the use of age bands and the absence of preferred underwriting.

The use of the insurance jargon used in the paragraph above is probably unfamiliar to most readers. All the more reason to talk to an insurance agent about your insurance needs. Not an author, or banker, or accountant. Talk to a trained professional.

The point of this essay is not that mortgage insurance is evil – in fact, it's far better to have something in place rather than nothing, and sometimes mortgage insurance actually works out okay. The point of this essay is that just because someone publishes something doesn't mean you can take it as gospel. Most especially, "expert opinions" from unqualified sources.

From November 2005

Wanted: A Few Good Suckers

As I AM HUNTING and pecking on the laptop, someone asks me what I am writing about this week. I gave her the overview of the material, and when I happened to mention that I was looking for an appropriate title for the essay, she suggested that I should call this one "Wanted: A Few Good Suckers."

My first reaction was to laugh, since at the time I had some lame, inoffensive working title like "Be Careful," but on further reflection I realized that "Wanted: A Few Good Suckers" was actually a damn good title. Not just because it is catchy, but more importantly, because I think it is accurate. And maybe sometimes people need to hear the unsanitized truth, even if it is not what they want to hear.

A little birdie told me that there are some guys coming to town, holding meetings, promising miracles.

I have no idea who these guys are. I wish I did so I could check into this some more. Not checking into it with the idea of investing, though. Checking into it so hopefully I could save somebody from making a $50,000 mistake.

Here's the pitch. They are going to turn $50,000 into $500,000 in 5 years. How? Offshore investing. Investing in what? Something to do with banks lending 300 bucks for every dollar on deposit.

No names, no documents, nothing of substance, really. The details are so sketchy that I really can't say with 100 percent certainty that it is an out-and-out rip-off. But that's only because the details are sketchy, not because the scheme is legitimate. This thing is so fishy that it has gills.

Here are the red flags that immediately leap out: First, to grow $50,000 to $500,000 in five years would require a rate of return that approaches 60 percent per year for 5 straight years. Yes, theoretically that could happen. Of course, theoretically there is a jolly old soul that lives at the North Pole and delivers toys to all the good little boys and girls. Theoretically.

Second, Offshore. Hello? When did "offshore" become a good word? When you hear "offshore" and "$50,000" in the same sentence, don't think "tax-haven", think "loose regulations," "murky financial statements," and "lack of enforcement." Think of the new boat that you just bought. For someone else.

Third, banks lending money out 300 times deposits. Sorry, this is not the magic wand that is going to make you wealthy, and for a couple of reasons. Yes, banks can and do lend out more money than they have on deposit. And the model works for the bank, the savers, and the borrowers as long as the bank lends prudently. 300 times is not prudent. Banks are profitable, not stupid.

Additionally, if the banks were to be so profitable, why would they need you? It's inconsistent. Think about it.

Seriously, I mean it. Take a pause, put the paper down for a moment, think about it, then come back and keep reading. If this grand plan is so wonderful, so fool-proof, so automatic, if these banks are so profitable, then why would they need you and your $50,000 at all? Why wouldn't they just keep the profit for themselves?

Fourth, the lack or forthrightness about who these guys are, what companies they work for, etc. Legitimate companies don't skulk into town. Legitimate companies that come to town to host a seminar will advertise the seminar. Legitimate companies have a prospectus or an offering memorandum, or at least a business card. Of course, all those things leave paper trails, which is a bad thing if you are in a shady business.

These are my concerns, and that's only based on what I know so far. If these guys approach you, then start asking questions. Get some stuff down on paper. Take it to your lawyer, accountant, or Certified Financial Planner. If it's legitimate, it can be verified.

Or don't believe me. Hey, it's your money. If you want to burn 50 thousand dollars, go nuts. Personally, if I had 50 thousand dollars that I wanted to go up in smoke I think that I would buy a whole whack of fireworks for Canada Day. At least that way you get to see some pretty colours. Oh well, to each his own.

P.T. Barnum said, "There is a sucker born every minute." Don't spend 50 grand to find out it's you.

Common Sense Isn't Common

WHEN IT COMES TO MAKING good financial decisions, a lot of it is just plain common sense. I just wish sometimes that common sense was a little more common.

Of course, everyone makes mistakes from time to time, but I'm not talking about something accidental, nor something that 20/20 hindsight reveals to be a bad idea. We all do those kinds of things from time to time. Stuff happens. We move on. Usually it's no big deal.

Here are a few examples of what I mean by common sense not always being common.

Eleven percent of Canadians plan on winning the lottery to fund part of their retirement. Now the odds of winning the jackpot in the 6/49 lottery are one in 13 million. And yet one in nine people are expecting that they are the guy. Does that make sense?

Does it make sense that someone you have never heard of will send you an email offering you a job making $4000 per week to work 2 hours a day from home? Or that he is a government official with access to a secret slush fund, willing to pay you 30% of the $120 million that he needs to get out of Nigeria? Or that you can make a return on your investment of 180% in just 3 weeks with no risk?

Why do people continue to respond to these emails? Do they make any sense?

Why do people put utmost faith in scam artists? If your brother asked you to write him a cheque for $100,000, you'd probably ask some questions. Maybe questions like; what's he planning to do with the money? How and when does he plan to pay you back? You know, little things like that.

If a guy would ask his own brother questions like this, why do people write cheques to strangers without asking these types of questions? Does it make sense to write a cheque to a stranger without asking the questions that you would ask a family member?

Last year the Canada Revenue Agency came down hard on schemes where people would put some money into a charitable donations arrangement, and get a tax deduction for many times the amount that they actually contributed.

The crazy thing was the CRA was very clear in trying to warn people off from these schemes. It was no secret. The CRA was loud and clear in stating that if you do this thing we will reassess you. Not only will you not get your deduction, but you will also be responsible for the fees and interest costs associated with not paying the proper amount of taxes that you legitimately owe. People did it anyway.

Does it make sense to write a cheque for $10,000 and then be able to deduct $40,000 in taxes? Especially after the CRA repeatedly said that these schemes stank like the milk you accidentally left on the counter before you left on a two-week trip?

I imagine that some readers are shaking their heads right now, thinking "I can't believe that people would actually do these things". But before you think things only happen to the other guy, here are a few examples of more common things that are also contrary to common sense.

One thing that people often do is to extrapolate a trend. They simply assume that the current trend will continue into the future.

When Elvis Presley died, back in 1977, there were 150 Elvis impersonators in the USA. By 1993 that number had swelled to 48,000. At that pace Elvis impersonators will account for a third of the world's population by 2019.

A world with 2 billion Elvis impersonators is clearly too silly to contemplate, but that's the type of results that you can end up with when you extrapolate the trend.

Unfortunately it is all too common for a person to want to jump on an investment after it has had a period of good performance. Let's say an investment just went up by 99 percent in the one year. Well, if the thing has already gone up by 99 percent, this may not be the right time to buy. But people do. They salivate over those mouth-watering returns, and they want a taste.

Trees don't grow to the sky, though. And it's not unusual for an investment that that has done spectacularly well in a short period of time to eventually fall. It's also not unusual for the fall to be proportionate to the rise.

Believe it or not, 99 percent in one year is not a made-up number. The Trimark Discovery Fund did it in 1999. And so a lot of people bought the Trimark Discovery Fund in early 2000. Even today, eight years later, that mutual fund is still down about 75% from 2000. Buying high is a tough way to make money.

People will extrapolate downward trends too. Let's say they have a good portfolio of blue chip investments that just happens to be down by 5 percent in a month. It's all too common for some people to think, "Man, if this keeps up I am going to be broke in 19 more months."

Now, bear in mind that I said that this was a good portfolio of blue chip investments. In previous essays I've told you that if you have junk in your portfolio, then your investments becoming cheaper does not necessarily make for an opportunity.

What it does make is cheap junk. That's called the cigar-butt method of investing, but that's a story for another day. Meanwhile, buying cheap junk is a tough way to make money.

The point is this; did it make sense to buy the Trimark Discovery Fund after it made 99 percent in 1999? Does it make sense to sell a good portfolio of blue chip investments if it goes down by 5 percent? Shouldn't we be buying low and selling high, not vice-versa?

Here's another example of something that doesn't make sense – and this one is probably the most common suspension of common sense – living outside your means.

Consumer debt is now around 30 percent of disposable personal income. Residential mortgage debt is around 90 percent of disposable household income. Add the two together, and the average guy has debt that's about 120 percent of his disposable income. That is insane.

Common sense is that you can't spend more than you make and have things end well. But the average guy is doing it. Spending more than they make. Digging themselves deeper and deeper.

Maybe a better name is uncommon sense! In any case, it needs to be put to work.

From January 2008

The Worst Month On Record

RECENTLY THE INVESTMENT FUNDS INSTITUTE OF CANADA reported that January 2008 was the worst month on record for redemptions of long-term mutual funds. This comes as no surprise to me.

Net redemptions in long-term investment funds were more than $4.3 billion in January. Now, part of the reason why this makes January the worst month on record is a function of the size of the industry.

Canadians have more than $670 billion invested in mutual funds, which is more than twice as much than just ten years ago. So, while the numbers are quite large in dollar terms, expressing the net redemptions in percentage terms paints a little different picture.

That's not the main reason that I'm not surprised though. I expected that, as a whole, Canadians weren't going to be putting a lot of money into long-term assets in the month of January for the simple reason that short-term investment performance of late has been disappointing.

This is not a brand new phenomenon. Investors have a long history of letting investment performance dictate their investment behaviour.

Going back to 1995, I looked at one-year performance numbers for the Toronto Stock Exchange and compared it to cash flows into mutual funds. The results were as expected. When the short-term performance numbers look good, people buy. When the short-term performance numbers aren't so rosy, people don't buy.

As an example, after back-to-back years of negative performance, 2002 was a great time to buy investments. And yet people stayed away in droves. Indeed, in the face of uncertainty, more people preferred to yank their money out of their long-term investments than to put more money to work at attractive prices.

In other words, rather than buying low, according to the oft-quoted (yet seldom followed) investing maxim of "buy low, sell high", people were selling low. It wasn't until 2003, after the TSX came up by 26 percent, that investors started buying again. But they came back at prices that were 26 percent higher than they could have gotten in 2002.

From an academic perspective, this is interesting for a couple of reasons. What makes someone who was a long-term investor just a few short months ago sell their long-term investments when we hit some turbulence?

And, rather than selling investments after they have temporarily declined, whatever happened to the idea of buying investments when they go on sale? If we liked the prospects for the Royal Bank when it was trading at $60, should we not like it even more when we can buy the same company for $50?

Canadians aren't the only investors that let investment performance dictate their behaviour. In the States, the research firm Dalbar looked at investor returns from 1984 to 2002, a time when the S&P500 went up by 12.22 percent per annum. During these prosperous times the average investor realized a paltry 2.57 percent annualized return.

Why the big gap? It's no mystery. Dalbar showed that investors tend to invest when the market is rising and pull out when it is declining. It's buy high, sell low and it clearly doesn't work. All these people had to do was sit still and they would have made an annualized return of 12.22 percent. But they didn't.

However people reconcile these contradictions to themselves, these people usually do not have a fundamentally solid reason for wanting to bail on long-term investments. They certainly can't realistically expect to be able to use the recent volatility as a predictor for future events.

In fact, noted investor Peter Lynch once said, "Thousands of experts study overbought indicators, oversold indicators, head-and-shoulder patterns, put-call ratios, the Fed's policy on money supply, foreign investment, the movement of the constellations through the heavens, and the moss on oak trees, and they can't predict markets with any useful consistency, any more than the gizzard squeezers could tell the Roman emperors when the Huns would attack."

Right or wrong, when markets get choppy a lot of investors head for the sidelines. Not everyone though. Warren Buffett is the World's Greatest

Investor. In the last 20 years Buffett's Berkshire Hathaway has appreciated by about 4,700 percent, about six times more than the Standard & Poor's 500 Index.

Buffett looks for great companies trading at attractive prices. In these choppy markets, Buffett is a buyer, not a seller.

Kraft Foods Inc., the world's second-biggest food maker, has declined about 15 percent during the past 12 months. Buffett started buying. Berkshire Hathaway is now the largest shareholder in Kraft.

GlaxoSmithKline, the world's second-largest pharmaceutical company, is down 26 percent. Buffett just bought 1.5 million shares, valued at about $65 million.

Wells Fargo & Co., the second-largest home lender in America, dropped 18 percent. Buffett already owned a large position in Wells Fargo. He bought more.

Buffett's performance from 1984 to 2002, the time frame looked at in the Dalbar study? Closer to 23 percent annualized.

The conclusion of the Dalbar study was this: "As market returns rose, investors poured cash into funds in an attempt to capitalize on high returns. When the market swung low, investors scrambled to redeem their shares before they lost additional money. In fact, the average investor remained invested in equity or fixed income funds for less than three years, their decision to sell or buy motivated primarily by swings in the market. The end result is investors buy high and sell low, and earn significantly less than the market indices. Investment return is far more dependent on investment behavior than on fund performance."

January 2008 being the worst month on record for redemptions of long-term mutual funds in Canada is just the latest example of something we've known for a long time. You can be like the investors in the Dalbar study, and make 2.57 percent.

Or you can be like Buffett, and take advantage of the opportunities that abound.

From February 2008

■ ■ ▪ ▪ ▪ ▪

Learning Golf from a Magazine

THE OTHER DAY I picked up a golf magazine. I play golf a few times a year, but not very well. I'd like to learn more about the how to play the game, and golf magazines are full of information, so what better way to learn, right?

And, admittedly, I have a lot to learn.

Take how you grip a golf club for example. I know that you are supposed to hold the golf club very gently as you swing. Some famous golf dude once said you hold the club as if you were holding a baby bird.

But I just don't get it. I don't understand how you can hold the club soft and hit the ball hard. That seems counter-intuitive to me. And just how hard does a guy hold a baby bird anyway? I've tried holding the club like I would hold a baby bird and it feels like the club is rotating in my hands as I swing. That can't be right.

So, aside from having a vague awareness of how you are supposed to grip the club, I really don't understand the proper grip, and consequently I swing the club the way that I feel should be swinging. I hang on tight, and let it rip.

I wish the grip was the only thing I needed to learn how to do properly. Unfortunately, the proper grip is just one of many things I need to learn.

For years my Dad has been telling me that the club face is open at the top of my swing. Either that, or he says the club face is closed at the top of the swing. Truth is, I can't remember exactly what it is about the club face, but apparently this is why I hook the ball.

My Dad golfs a lot, and he keeps telling me how I can fix this club-face-at-the-top-of-my-swing thing. But I really don't know what he is trying to tell me. As far as I know I am swinging the club the way he tells me to, but apparently to him it looks like I have the same old crappy swing, and I am still not doing it right.

Frankly, it's kind of hard to figure out what he is trying to tell me. And since I don't really understand what he is saying, I don't really listen, and I end up continuing to swing the way that I always have. And continuing to consistently hook the ball.

Because I don't know any better, I keep doing things on the golf course based on how I think I should be doing things instead of how I actually should be doing things. Consequently, my results are sporadic and do not improve, and I get frustrated at my lack of success.

But you know what my real problem is? It isn't my grip, and it isn't the club face at the top of my swing. My real problem is that I don't know what I don't know.

I played a little of that virtual golf this winter, and one of the cool parts about it is that you can see a video of your golf swing. I've never seen my own golf swing before. I have this mental image of my swing as being graceful, balanced and powerful. But the swing that I see in my head looks nothing at all like the swing that I see on the video.

So, after reading the golf magazine, do you think I am a better golfer? Nope, my game hasn't changed one bit. I'm not even sure that a person can learn how to golf from a magazine. Sure I might pick up some useful tips, but how can a golf magazine know what I need?

There is a lot of information out there, but how do I know which information is right for me? So I am going to get some golf lessons. And I am going to get them from a golf professional, not from a magazine.

By the way, this essay isn't really about my golf game. Just as I won't learn much about the game of golf from a magazine, you probably won't learn all that you need to know about financial planning from a magazine either.

If you want to get a grip on your finances, don't blindly do what you think you should be doing. What if you are wrong? Have you ever been wrong before? Maybe your finances deserve a second opinion?

If you want to understand what is going on, don't quit listening to people who know what they are talking about. If you keep doing things in a way that hasn't really worked in the past, why would you not want to figure out how to do it better?

Find out what you don't know. Talk to a professional financial planner.

From May 2012

When Optimism Becomes Gullibility

WHEN PEOPLE DECIDE they are going to invest their money in something, they are going to be optimistic about the outcome. After all, it's pretty rare that someone would invest in something expecting poor results.

Sometimes people get so optimistic about an idea that they are willing to suspend common sense and believe almost anything about the idea. Some even go as far as to believe in things that sound too good to be true. Unfortunately, more often than not, that's completely correct.

The reality is that there are people who prey on gullibility. There always have been.

Back in the 1920s there was a crook by the name of Charles Ponzi, who promised phenomenal investment returns. Investors were allegedly able to double their money in a short period of time. And initially, that's exactly what happened.

The early investors actually did see wonderful "returns". The word gets around that this Ponzi guy is on to something, and now the money starts pouring in.

The only problem was that it was a massive fraud.

Ponzi used the money from the newest investors to fund the "returns" for previous investors. What this means is that the early investors in the Ponzi scheme actually can prosper. But if they do, they do it at the expense of the later investors.

Schemes like this inevitably fail. Here's an example. Let's say that Ponzi, or someone like him, needs two investors to fund the "returns" for every one of the few early people who actually do make some money. So if he has 10 investors, he needs to go and find 20 new people to pay out his initial 10 people. But now he needs 40 new people to pay out the people in the round of 20. And, following that, he needs 80 people to pay out the people in the round of 40. And so on.

Well, after only just 20 more rounds of this, the fraudster would need 83 million people to keep this thing going. Obviously that isn't going to happen. Without exception, the number of new investors eventually dries up and the scheme comes crashing down.

In Ponzi's case, about 40,000 people invested a total of about $15 million. But only about a third of that money went to the "investors."

Victims of such schemes are not necessarily unintelligent or naïve. Indeed, in the Ponzi case, a significant percentage of the Boston police force were victimized.

Nowadays this scheme is so well known that Ponzi's name is synonymous with it. But, even though the scheme is no secret, it continues to suck people in. Just within the last few months the latest version of the Ponzi scheme was revealed.

Bernie Madoff was a legendary figure in the investment world. A former Chairman of the NASDAQ stock exchange, he was a well-known and respected asset manager in the United States. His clients were among the who's who in the business and entertainment worlds.

Supposedly his advanced investment strategies were able to produce steady returns regardless of market conditions. Over time he developed an exclusive clientele of very well-heeled individuals, institutions, and charitable foundations.

Unfortunately Madoff's apparent ability to generate steady returns came not from special insight into investing in a dynamic environment, but because he robbed Peter to pay Paul. By Madoff's own admission it was "one big lie"; the biggest Ponzi scheme in history, coming in at an unbelievable $50 billion.

Like all con games, the perpetrator gains the victim's trust, and then exploits that trust. It would be nice to think that we live in a world where you can always take what people tell you at face value, but that's simply not the case. Just because someone tells you something doesn't make it true, perhaps especially so when this person is trying to persuade you to trust them with your money.

The hard part is that you might really want to believe this person. But simply wanting to believe it doesn't make it true.

There are seemingly an unlimited number of scoundrels out there. Recently I began counting how many schemes show up in my email inbox. I'm averaging about 15 per week.

There are inheritances from relatives that you never heard of. Princesses in Third World countries that need to smuggle money out of their country so their corrupt government doesn't get their hands on it. Chinese manufacturers that need a local contact to process the money from product orders. Massive lottery winnings that require prepayment of a processing fee and/or local tax. Banks that need you to validate your account information. All of these things are bogus.

The only limit to such schemes is the culprit's imagination, but they have one thing in common. These are crimes of persuasion.

I'm not sure if there are reliable figures out there for how lucrative these crimes are. Nobody likes being a sucker, so there is a large amount of this type of stuff that never gets reported. Whatever the figure is, it's a very big number, of that there is no doubt.

Smart people can get duped too. Madoff's victims were neither inexperienced nor simple-minded. But they were trusting.

So how can a person steer clear of these illicit schemes? One very good way is to heed the warnings of people who know. If the Canada Revenue Agency says a tax shelter is bogus well in advance of an actual audit you probably should listen. If a regulatory agency has someone on their disciplined persons list you should probably pay attention. If you Google something, and you get 1000 hits that include the word "scam", you should probably give that appropriate consideration. When the preponderance of information available is trying to warn you off, you should take note.

A second clear indicator is that legitimate investments come with paperwork. Normally quite a lot of paperwork, as a matter of fact. If there is no documentation it is quite possible that is because there is no investment in the first place.

Your Mom probably told you that if it sounds too good to be true, it probably is. She was right.

From March 2009

There Is No Magic Wand

THERE IS A MYTH out there, sometimes propagated by some mainstream financial media, that there are simple shortcuts for wealth creation. That's simply not true.

Now there are some schemes out there that are pure fiction, but that's not what I am talking about here.

I'm talking about ideas that are solid for what they are, but with the telling of them they gain larger-than-life status until eventually some people believe they are something that they are not. And what they are not is some magic wand that, with a mere wave, makes all good things come true.

Some financial publications would have you believe that if you follow some simplistic formula then all will be well. Unfortunately the financial world is seldom so clear-cut that simplistic formulas have much utility. The bottom line is that, despite all those magazine articles claiming an easy path to riches, there is no secret formula or other shortcut to financial success.

There have been a number of investment ideas suggested as easily implemented, can't miss solutions. In the last few years index funds, exchange traded funds, income trusts and dividends have all had their cult followings. Sure, these ideas are fine for what they are, but they are certainly not a miracle cure-all that will solve all problems.

There is nothing intrinsically wrong with any of these things, mind you. The trouble can come from the false sense of security that accompanies from some pundit's endorsement, and the potential misapplication of the idea.

Bad things can happen if you take an idea, even a good idea, out of context. Even something as normal and natural as oxygen can be a bad thing in the wrong circumstance. Just introduce oxygen to a fire and you'll see what I mean.

It seems like dividend-paying stocks are the current investment that is fashionable with the miracle-cure crowd. Again, there is nothing wrong with the idea of receiving dividends on your investments. In fact, a nice dividend yield is a very favourable attribute for an investment. But it remains just one part of the big picture. Simply paying a dividend won't make a stock the right investment for all people.

Lately there have been companies that pay attractive dividends that have had their share prices come down significantly. As an example, you could take a look at just about any large cap financial services company, many of which have seen their share prices get chopped in half. Getting a healthy dividend is great, but that benefit will be dwarfed if your investment is suddenly worth half as much.

I don't even mind too much that, all of a sudden, people are interested in dividends again. Over time, dividends can be a significant part of an investment's total return. It's just that the dividend itself doesn't guarantee a successful outcome.

I think an idea that has even more of a potential for inappropriate use is the apparent fascination with taking shortcuts on constructing an investment portfolio.

Recently I heard of a "Two-Minute Portfolio." In my mind the idea of spending two minutes a year on your financial future is comedic. But there it is. And someone is going to take this at face value.

The idea behind the Two-Minute Portfolio is to "annually invest equal amounts in the two largest dividend-paying names in each of the ten sectors of the Canadian market." Well, that sounds great. Except...

What about all the people who shouldn't be 100 percent in stocks? What about all the things that aren't represented by the 10 sectors that happen to exist in Canada? What about when lousy investments happen to be big, such as Nortel? What about if we like the prospects for some investments, and we don't want to sell them after they have come down in price? What about the guy who is trying to do this with a small portfolio and now has up to 40 brokerage fees to pay each year? What about the taxation of a non-registered portfolio that has that kind of turnover? Etcetera.

Often these types of quick-fix proposals suggest that the low-cost nature is a competitive advantage. To which I say, when you look at your total all-in costs, is it really cheaper in the first place? Often a person will be surprised at just how much they are paying for their "low cost" idea.

But perhaps more important, when are people going to realize that cheap isn't a synonym for good? I can drink cheap tequila, but that doesn't make it good for me.

Unfortunately, you won't see these types of journalists writing a column that says "Listen, friend, you've got some talents, but for the most part you don't cut your own hair, fix your own teeth, perform your own mammograms, represent yourself in legal actions, repair your own transmission, replace your own water main, fall your own dangerous trees, or star in your own Hollywood blockbuster. So why do you think that you can plan your own finances?"

"Sure exceptional people can do it. Chances are, that's not you. Go see a professional. Be aware that, just like not all barbers, dentists, doctors, lawyers, mechanics, plumbers, tree-fallers and movie stars are world-class, not everyone who calls themselves a financial planner is exceptional. This is the 6 step financial planning process. It's a good starting spot to help you figure out whom you should hire to plan your finances. That way you can focus on the stuff that you are good at."

A column like that wouldn't sell magazines though. So the myth that investing is easy and can be competently done by amateurs in minutes continues to be perpetuated.

From March 2009

Market Cycles and Investor Emotions

CANADIAN INVESTORS HAVE a disturbing habit of doing exactly the wrong thing at the wrong time.

If you were to look at statistics of money flows into mutual funds you can actually do a pretty good job of estimating what is going on in the markets. Money pours in when the market is hot. When the markets are down, investors panic and the money tap turns off.

Which, of course, is exactly the opposite of what people should do if investment decisions were rational.

Here's an example: In August of 1998, when the Asian Flu currency crisis caused a short-lived but dramatic market dip, investors stopped investing. The markets recovered, naturally, and went on a spectacular one-year tear. Those people who panicked prior to the recovery did not participate in the recovery.

In 2000, when the markets were near the peak of the bubble, money poured in to the tune of 1.3 billion dollars in domestic equity funds in the month of February alone. Of course, all of this hot money ended up being invested just in time to take the long, painful ride to where we are today.

Ultimately it comes down to this. Investor behavior typically leads to bad decisions on timing. I have been harping away at this for three years now, because the message doesn't change, even during this exceptional bear market. If anything, the message gets louder.

The lower things go, the better the opportunities are going forward. Sure, it's kind of a drag when you see those quarterly statements and discover that the recovery hasn't kicked in yet, but that's the way it is. To complete the buy-low, sell-high equation people actually have to buy low.

As markets go through their constant cycle of growth, peak, decline, bottom and back to growth people's emotions move in tandem. They are optimistic when things are on the way up, euphoric when markets are near the top, fearful when things slide, and eventually even depressed when things bottom out.

Get off the emotional roller coaster. It doesn't help anybody, and it hurts most people. Just look at the cash flows into investments. Markets are hot, people are thrilled, and money pours in. Right at the point of maximum financial risk, they get excited. Conversely, markets are down in the dumps, people are despondent and they don't invest. Right at the point of maximum financial opportunity, they miss the opportunity.

I frequently take part in a financial advisor town hall. It's kind of a free-for-all, where advisors shoot around topics of interest, and the discussion can get pretty lively.

One fellow put forward the topic of his own 90-day strategy given the Iraq situation. Which I thought was absolutely ludicrous. This fellow, who claims to have a long-term outlook, is thinking about how the next 90 days are going to play out. You see, he is thinking that the stuff with the best potential for the future is exactly the same stuff that has already done well. He has been suckered into that very same trap of putting money in investments that have already had a good run, and neglecting investments that are beaten up.

This fellow didn't see the irony in the contradiction. He thinks he has a long-term focus, but is thinking about the next 90 days. Just like all of the other people who sold low in 1998 or bought high in 2000.

The truth is nobody knows with certainty exactly how the next 90 days will play out. No one knows if the markets will slide even farther in the next 90 days. No one knows if markets will take off tomorrow.

What we do know, as history has shown over and over and over, is that five or ten years from now things are probably going to look much better. Get off the roller coaster, and have faith in the long-term.

From February 2003

The Next Big Thing

ONE OF MY BUDDIES called me up the other day, looking to buy $7000 of "the next big thing" that his coworkers are talking about. When I found which stock he wanted to buy I gave him the Charlie Munger line: Just give the seven grand to me. I don't mean invest it through me; I mean give it to me as a gift. He's not going to make any money whether he buys the stock or whether he gives the money away, but at least in the latter case he will have my enduring gratitude.

It was a penny mining stock that had gone up in price a little. He asked if the stock was really that bad. Yep, it was.

I asked him how he thought that he would make money on this potential investment. As it turns out, he didn't actually know why the stock might appreciate. His buddies were saying that it was going to go up, and the stock actually had gone up some recently, but the reasons that would drive this expected future growth were not clear.

On further investigation, the reason that the stock had gone up in price is that the company had just emerged from creditor protection. On top of that, they had recently closed the mine. And, believe it or not, that's only part of this company's problems.

Why somebody would put good money in bad investments is something that baffles me, and yet many people are doing just this, in search of the next big thing.

Earlier today I was in a waiting room that had the ubiquitous magazine collection on the coffee table. One of the magazine's happened to be a venture capital magazine, and I shuddered to read the cover story "100 companies to invest in NOW," with the accent on the NOW.

Apparently the sole criteria that the magazine used to determine which companies that people should invest in was one-year returns, and so their top pick to invest in NOW was a company that was trading at 6 cents a year ago, and traded most recently at $1.42, for a quoted one-year return of 2,150%.

Ahh, if only investing was so easy. Pick the one that went up the most last year and relax. No reason to let common sense get in the way of the next big thing.

But, unfortunately, that's not the way the world works. Here's where we have to inject a little reality into the essay.

The next big thing is not necessarily next, nor big, nor even much of a thing. Remember the technology mania of the late 1990's? How many of those Internet IPOs are still breathing today? For every colossal success story there are dozens, and probably hundreds of disappointments, if not outright failures. Chances are that your crystal ball is no better at showing the future than the next guys.

And, you probably missed the boat anyway. By the time that the story is touted in the Globe and Mail, and the company CEO is on everybody's A list, it is probably too late; the easy money has already been made, and the stock is overpriced.

Why would the next big thing be overpriced? Because it's always over-priced. After all, it's the next big thing. Everybody wants a piece of the action.

And even if the next big thing turns out to be successful, that doesn't mean it will make any money for shareholders. Take satellite radio for instance. Another friend of mine got one of these for Christmas. The product is pretty slick, but will the company make any money? It's too soon to tell.

Now here's the good news – you don't need the next big thing to be a successful investor. You can concentrate on fundamentals. Profitability. Price. Free cash flow. Debt to equity. Strength of management. Barriers to entry. Industry outlook. Real stuff that can even be measured, not just faith and hope.

Personally, I'll always take a wonderful business at a fair price over the next big thing.

From June 2005

PART THREE

When Playing It Safe Isn't

It's not the iceberg that you see that sinks your ship;
it's the one that you don't.

■ ■ ■ ■ ■ ■

What Is Safe?

RECENTLY SOMEONE SUGGESTED to me that I should write about "what is safe" when it comes to investments. No doubt that there are some people, after seeing their last quarter's investment statement, who will agree that "what is safe" is a topical theme.

This essay isn't merely about short-term market volatility, however. It's more about how you need to look at investments in order to have a successful investing experience.

Still, the topic of volatility is worth discussing. And with the volatility that we have seen over the last few years, I have had this type of conversation with plenty of people.

The bottom line is that many people plain hate the fact that they just opened up one more nasty quarterly statement, in what seems like a never-ending stream of nasty quarterly statements, and it's getting pretty irksome.

Through those conversations, I have noticed an interesting thing. Sometimes people want to make sure that I get it when they tell me that they hate seeing quarterly statements showing depressing market turmoil. It's probably because my message to them never changes – stay focused on your objectives, buy quality investments when they get cheap, hold them for the long term, etc. – that sometimes people will say something interesting to me.

They'll say "I know it's not a lot of money, but..."

I guess people say this because they want to make sure that I know that it's their money and to them, regardless of the dollar amount, it's serious money. Interestingly, I have had people say that about a few thousand dollars, but also a few hundred thousand dollars.

Friends, you don't need to preface the fact that you hate "losing" money with any type of qualifying statement. Everybody hates losing money. I get it.

So when a guy like me says something like "stay focused on your objectives," it's not a question of failing to grasp the need for safety in troubling times. Everyone has some measure of that need.

The real question is, "what is safe?"

Is going to cash safe, when we have astounding budget deficits and inflation eroding purchasing power? Is going to gold safe, when it's got all the trappings of the next great asset bubble? Are bonds safe, when interest rates near-zero now and hikes inevitable? Is it safe to avoid equities now that they are trading with both prices and dividend yields not seen in decades? And does the volatility of last quarter's statement really compromise the safety of someone who owns quality investments and has a long-term investment horizon?

You see, sometimes what seems like a good and comfortable idea can actually be rife with danger.

Imagine that you are a greenhorn in the north, and you are out in the bush during the extremes of winter. All the old greybeards have told you that, whatever you do, don't fall asleep in the bitter, numbing cold. But you are tired, and your fingers aren't working so good. Your toes fell asleep long ago, the wind is carving right through you, and all you want to do is lie down and rest for a while. It seems like such a good and comfortable idea... Unless, of course, you freeze to death.

Still, this popular quest for investment "safety" – perhaps most commonly defined as, "whatever it is that I have now, get me out" – is getting some real traction. Some people are seeing danger at every turn. That's completely normal. If you go looking for danger, you can find reasons to think danger is about to pounce.

I saw an interview with a race car driver following the fatal crash that took the life of driver Dan Wheldon. He said, "Dan Wheldon's death is a true tragedy and a loss for the sport and anyone who knew him. I would be lying if I said his death didn't make me pause to think about how much I am willing to risk to be in the sport. That said, if someone came to me tomorrow and offered me a job driving Indy Cars I would say yes."

And then he said something that stuck with me. He said, "While I don't have the numbers to back this up, you may be able to make the case that your odds of getting injured driving along the highway every day for a 9-5 job are higher than those of getting injured in a racecar accident. Death is everywhere if you look for it, so I just don't look for it."

This type of thing is also true when it comes to investing. You may perceive excessive risk when it comes to dramatic events, and you may underestimate real risk when it comes to more commonplace events, and if you let the risk become a distraction you won't be able to accomplish your goals.

So let's talk about what is safe. Right now high quality equity investments are trading at prices not seen in years.

Here's an analogy. Let's say that you could buy real estate today, and pay 1990 prices. Would that interest you?

Well, I'm afraid that you can't buy real estate at 1990 prices right now, but these are the types of opportunities that we have in the equity markets. And, my friends, buying high quality assets at cheap prices is completely congruent with the idea of safety.

The bottom line is that part of being safe with your money is making sure that your investments, and your investment behaviour, is consistent with your objectives. Sometimes that might make you uncomfortable. But remember, what appears to be risk – and what appears to be risk-free – can be deceiving. When it comes to investments and safety, much like our greenhorn lying down in the snow for a rest, what seems good and comfortable might actually be quite dangerous.

So, again, what is safe? Is going to cash safe, when we have astounding budget deficits and inflation eroding purchasing power? Is going to gold safe, when it's got all the trapping of the next great asset bubble? Are bonds safe, when interest rates near-zero now and hikes inevitable? Is it safe to avoid equities now that they are trading with both prices and dividend yields not seen in decades? And does the volatility of last quarter's statement really compromise the safety of someone who owns quality investments and has a long-term investment horizon?

From October 2011

How Do You React to a Big Price Drop?

It's early Monday morning, and I'm dog tired. People who know me know that I'm not a morning person at the best of times. I get to the office, and my associate Meagan has a great big ear-to-ear grin on her face.

In my foggy mental state I immediately grow suspicious. Why is she so energetic so early? Something is happening, no doubt about it.

I ask her what's up, and she tells me that the Toronto Stock Exchange Composite Index is down 490 points already this morning. Now this is happening on the heels of some other big drops that have recently occurred in this young year.

I ask her why would the TSX going down 490 points make her smile. I mean, I know what I think about the TSX dropping 490 points, and I even know how I think she's going to answer, but I'm curious about just what she thinks about the current state of affairs.

Meagan says, "It's exciting."

I say, "Exciting how? Scary exciting, or opportunity exciting?"

"Both," she says.

Meagan is smart. It is both. It is scary, but it is also an opportunity.

Here's a famous Warren Buffett quote about the opportunity, and it comes in the form of a short quiz: "If you plan to eat hamburgers throughout your life and are not a cattle producer, should you wish for higher or lower prices for beef? Likewise, if you are going to buy a car from time to time but are not an auto manufacturer, should you prefer higher or lower car prices? These questions, of course, answer themselves."

"But now for the final exam: If you expect to be a net saver during the next five years, should you hope for a higher or lower stock market during that period?"

"Many investors get this one wrong. Even though they are going to be net buyers of stocks for many years to come, they are elated when stock prices rise and depressed when they fall. In effect, they rejoice because prices have risen for the "hamburgers" they will soon be buying."

"This reaction makes no sense. Only those who will be sellers of equities in the near future should be happy at seeing stocks rise. Prospective purchasers should much prefer sinking prices."

Now here's the scary part. Right now, there is a lot of uncertainty out there, and this is not the time for uncertain investments. The plain truth is that some stuff isn't going to recover. When we talk about buying hamburgers it should go without saying that we are talking about tasty and nutritious stuff that is on sale, not buying mad cows.

And even with the good quality stuff I can't tell you when the sun will come out again. Even the optimistic people are saying that it may take a bit. We are not talking days here, and probably not weeks either, but rather months.

So is that cause for consternation? Only if you have uncertain investments. Or if you are not properly diversified. Or if you have a short time frame, but hold long-term investments. And if you are in one of these situations then hard choices may need to be made.

Otherwise, though, only those who will be sellers of equities in the near future should be happy at seeing stocks rise. Prospective purchasers should much prefer sinking prices.

As for me, I'm as happy as a kid at Christmas. I'm going to be speaking to a lot of people over the next few weeks about topping up their retirement savings plans, and these are the type of market conditions that are good for buying quality investments at distressed prices. And that, my friends, is the recipe for long-term investment success.

From January 2008

Spring Clearance Sale

A LITTLE WHILE AGO someone asked me how I was positioning people in the light of the dramatic market volatility that we saw at the start of the year.

I told him that I was considering getting one of those signs with the fluorescent letters for the front lawn, and on it I was going to say "Spring Clearance Sale. Toronto Stock Exchange 15% off. Limited Time Offer."

The part about the fluorescent sign I said in fun, but I'm not joking about the message.

Most people get it backwards when it comes to investing. When the markets go on sale, as they inevitably do from time to time, people get apprehensive rather than embracing the opportunity. There's a reason for that, and I'll speak to that in a minute.

Think about this for a second, though. If we were talking about any other product: rubber boots, motorcycle trailers, airline tickets, pizza, Dora the Explorer DVDs, whatever… if these items were priced at a 15% discount you would expect an increased demand for them. Investments, on the other hand, are the only thing that I can think of where demand falls when the price gets cheaper.

The simplistic reason why people will buy boots and DVDs and so on when they are on sale, but be less excited about buying investments on sale, is the difference in the nature of the products. After all, pizza and investing are different things. The real reason, though, goes much deeper.

Usually people actually go through a completely different thought process when it comes to buying investments than they do when they buy other things. Unfortunately, it's not a thought process that is conducive to making good decisions.

Most of the time, most people make rational decisions when it comes to purchasing everything except investments. If you need a motorcycle trailer, and they go on sale, you'd be inclined to go out and buy one. That's logical.

When it comes to investments, however, it's far more common for people to suspend logic, and make decisions based on emotion. Money is, after all, an emotional thing. Money is what allows you to do the things that you want to do – get the house that fits your lifestyle, educate your kids, retire in comfort and with security. It's natural that a person would get worked up if he thought that important things like that might be compromised.

There is a problem with thinking emotionally though. It makes people act counterproductively.

If I were to go stand on the street corner and ask the first 50 people that I saw whether they thought that it was a better idea to buy something at a low price or to buy it at a higher price, I would expect all 50 people would say that paying a low price is clearly better. Indeed, the superiority of paying a low price is so self-evident, I wouldn't be surprised if some people would be inclined to question my mental faculties. After all, why would anybody want to pay an inflated price for something?

But then if my next question to these same 50 people was whether they intended to take advantage of the current stock market volatility and buy quality investments at unusually attractive prices, I would expect that only a minority of people would remain consistent with their answer to the first question.

Right now the markets are down from where they were earlier. People understand that it makes more sense to buy at a lower price than at a higher price. And yet they find some way to rationalize their decision to not take advantage of prices that one day we will look back on and say "I wish I had bought then".

People might say "Things are just too uncertain". Or they might say "The U.S. may be heading into a recession." Often people will say "I'm just going to wait until things turn around a bit", as if somebody was going to ring a giant bell to let us know just when that would be.

Whatever words are used to rationalize the decision, what people are really saying is "I'm scared that I'm going to lose." I understand that. And I'm telling you that there is no giant bell that goes off to inform people when is the best time to make an investment.

If you have a diversified portfolio of wonderful investments and a long investment horizon, then the inevitable bouts of market uncertainty are not the times to fear, but rather the times to rationally embrace the opportunity. Buy low, remember.

I'm not talking about blindly throwing money into the markets. I'm talking about what works. Diversification. Buy wonderful investments and hold them for the long-term. Buy even more of them when the prices get cheaper. Dollar Cost Averaging. Ideas that will turn volatility into opportunity.

Spring Clearance Sale. Toronto Stock Exchange 15% off. Limited Time Offer.

From February 2008

They Just Keep Popping Up

THE OTHER DAY I realized that I don't just have a house in the country. I have a dandelion farm. And I've got a bumper crop this year.

I can mow the lawn and the dandelions are back in all their glory almost before the lawnmower engine is cold. I've got this beautifully cut lawn with grass that is 2 inches high, and towering over it is this miniature forest of dandelions that are 6 inches high. How is it that I can cut all the grass, yet miss all the dandelions?

Investment scams are like dandelions. They keep popping up, and until you pull them out by the roots, they just keep coming back.

And, like dandelions, investment scams are right here in our own backyards. There are people getting ripped off right here, right now.

These aren't naïve people that are getting ripped off either. Many of them are smart and sophisticated. And they are still falling victim to scams.

Investment scams come in many colours, and the problem is so pervasive that the British Columbia Securities Commission has set up a special website to educate people. It's at www.investright.org.

The thing about scams is that the good ones appear to be legitimate ventures. You might even know some of the people who vouch for the scam. That doesn't necessarily mean that these people are the perpetrators of the scam. People who claim the scam is valid are often innocent victims themselves, who haven't realized that people are going to get ripped off.

If you are approached by someone who wants your money there are a number of red flags that can alert you that something might be amiss.

One of the most obvious red flags is the promise of guaranteed high returns with no risk. High-return, no-risk investments simply don't exist.

Risk and return are inevitably linked. You can have high-return investments. You can have no-risk investments. You can't have both at the same time. If someone tells you different, hang up the phone.

Another tactic used by scammers is to pressure you to act fast to take advantage of inside information. This is bogus. If they really did have inside information, securities laws prohibits them from sharing it with you anyway. But they don't have inside information; they are just using high-pressure tactics to get you to make a snap decision. A decision that you will come to regret.

Offshore investing is another popular tactic. Usually this comes with some sort of reference to a tax haven. Don't fall for it. What offshore investing really means is that you can wave goodbye to your money, because it's taking a trip and it's not coming back.

Another familiar pitch is to profit like the experts. The claim is of secret techniques, known only by a select group of elite, well-connected, rich dudes. It's a lie. There is no clandestine prime bank market. The only secret here is whether the guy who steals your money is planning on buying the Porsche or the Mercedes.

Perhaps the trickiest tactic of all – your friends are taking advantage of this great investment opportunity. You think that if your friends think its okay, then it must be legitimate. There are a couple of reasons why this tactic is very effective. You trust your friends. But also you don't want to miss out on something that they are into.

Here are some examples of common scams.

The affinity scam occurs in a group setting, such as a religious group, club or association, or an ethnic group. The scammer will gain trust by joining the group. Once they are accepted into the group there is a natural level of trust because of the common interest shared by members of the group. I've seen affinity fraud on numerous occasions.

The Ponzi or pyramid scheme promises high returns, but inevitably fails. The people who get in early see some results, but those results come from the funds of other victims, not from true wealth creation. More and more participants are needed to support the pyramid until it ultimately collapses. And pyramid schemes always collapse; it's a mathematical certainty. That's why pyramid schemes are illegal. It's an absolute certainty that eventually people are defrauded.

The West African letter scam has been around since before people had email. Postage is expensive though, so nowadays you'll see this one in your email inbox, not your post office box. The scammers allege that due to complications your help is needed moving millions of dollars, for which you will be richly rewarded. Just delete these. Don't even bother reading them, unless you are amused by spelling and grammatical errors. Trust me, the only time that people you have never heard of are going to give you money is if you are manning a Salvation Army kettle at Christmas time, and they don't need to email you to do that.

There are some things that you can do to protect yourself.

Know yourself. Determine your investment goals, your risk tolerance, and the limits of your own investment knowledge.

Know the proposed investment. Understand where the return on your investment is going to come from, the liquidity, and the risk. Does this fit with your financial objectives? What information is publically available? Is the management competent and reputable?

Know your advisor. Check their qualifications. Are they registered to sell securities? Have there been any disciplinary actions against them? Can they provide references?

Understand the pressure tactics used by scammers. Resist these tactics. Be suspicious of payments made directly to individuals or their private companies. Be suspicious of advice to cash out of your current investments in favour of something that you have never heard of until five minutes ago.

Finally, get everything in writing. And if your instinct is that something is just not right, trust your instincts.

From June 2009

The Tale of the Razor Blade

WHILE I VERY MUCH enjoy writing these essays, my real job is to help people make smart decisions about their money; decisions that are consistent with their financial objectives, so that they can move closer to their Great Goals in life.

Today I have a message for the people whose financial objectives include the long term accumulation of wealth.

It's time to buy.

I'll tell you more about why it's time to buy in a moment, but first I want to elaborate on this notion of financial objectives. Far too often people take their eye off the ball, and lose track of why they are doing something in the first place.

So when I talk about the long-term accumulation of wealth, what I am really talking about are things like retiring with dignity by maintaining your standard of living in a rising cost world, or providing a post-secondary education for your loved ones that gives them the building blocks for a successful life, or leaving a meaningful legacy to the charities that are closest to your heart. These are examples of Great Goals.

With the headlines of the day it's so easy to lose focus from your own Great Goals in life. But here's the thing – that last statement could be made on virtually every single day since the invention of headlines. There is always some white noise distraction happening somewhere. With very seldom exceptions, that's all the financial headlines are; a distraction. In twenty years nobody is going to care about what happened in the last 30 days.

So for the people whose long-term objectives include wealth accumulation – people who have the eye on the ball and are focused on achieving their Great Goals – it's time to buy.

I don't mean buy indiscriminately, mind you. I wouldn't be interested in considering owning shares of Facebook unless they were trading 90 percent cheaper, and I think anyone who loads up on fixed income investments right now is likely flirting with disaster.

What I mean is that for people whose long-term objectives include the accumulation of wealth, the time to accumulate larger positions in quality investments is right now, while prices remain attractive.

I could talk about price/earnings ratios and dividend yields, and all the other valuation measures that scream out, "Stocks are on sale!" But rather than overcomplicating things I am going to talk about Gillette Fusion Pro-Glide razor blades.

The other day I was in the store, picking up some stuff. I had recently bought a Gillette Fusion ProGlide razor, and now I needed some blades to go with it.

Now, if you don't happen to be a consumer of men's razor blades, I'll fill you in on how this racket works. The razor they'll sell you cheap. But the razor won't do you much good without the blades, and it's the blades that are costly.

So, choking back my disbelief at the price, I chucked a pack of 4 blades into the cart and proceeded with my shopping. But, to my delight, when I got to the checkout I found the very same packs of razor blades for ten dollars cheaper!

For this story to really sink in, you need to know a little about my current appearance. On a lark, I haven't fully shaved since last November. I have worn a goatee for years, and on one lazy Sunday in November rather than trimming the goatee, I just thought to myself "I wonder what will happen if I don't shave." Well, you can see for yourself what happens on the Brad Brain Financial Planning Inc. Facebook page. It's a fashion tragedy.

So, even though my current demand for razor blades is sparse, when I got to the checkout and I saw them marked down by ten dollars a pack, what do you think I did? Obviously I bought some. In fact, I got greedy, and I bought the entire display. Buying quality products when they are on sale just makes sense.

So when I had the chance to buy razor blades on sale I didn't lament the price that blades used to sell for. I didn't ponder whether they would get cheaper in the future. It didn't even cross my mind that I would sell any previously purchased razor blades at the current discounted price.

All that happened was that I needed razor blades; they went on sale; so I bought a bunch.

Guess what? Investors should look at the investments they need in precisely the same way that I looked at razor blades. Precisely the same way.

Some nervous people might say, "Sure markets are cheap, but what about all this fear and uncertainty?"

Exactly! It's that very same fear and uncertainty that allows us to buy quality investments at discounted prices. And, as Warren Buffett says "We simply attempt to be fearful when others are greedy and to be greedy only when others are fearful."

So what are you waiting for? The price of razor blades to go up? Go get your chequebook out of the drawer and get on in to see your financial advisor before the big sale on quality investments ends.

If you don't buy when things are cheap, what are you going to do? Wait until the price goes up and buy then?

From July 2012

I'm Probably Going to Say
I Told You So

I'M NOT REALLY MUCH of an "I told you so" kind of guy. It's rare that I will smugly gloat about being right.

But I am not so sure that I will be able to hold back this time. I'm probably going to have to say "I told you so" when equity markets soar and fixed income investments stall.

Let's be clear here. When I use the word probably, it's not because I have any uncertainty at all in my mind about how this will play out. I am simply referring to whether or not I can restrain myself from reminding all the people that are going to be wrong that I told them that they were wrong well in advance.

You see, right now "everyone" says equities are risky. But bear in mind that in the past "everyone" thought that the world was flat. "Everyone" thought that the sun revolved around the earth. "Everyone" thought that the Titanic was unsinkable.

In their time, almost "everyone" held these ideas to be self-evident and indisputable. But then, of course, and despite these conventional beliefs of the day, there is the world as it actually exists.

What we have at the moment is a nervous herd of investors, convinced that equities are "risky", and about to miss out on one of the great investing opportunities of their lifetime.

We have people who are ridiculously overweight in cash and fixed income investments at the bottom of an interest rate cycle.

We have people shunning investments in the great companies of the world, even though these companies are trading at prices that are dirt cheap.

"Everyone" is fearful of some unprecedented economic collapse, even though corporate earnings are at all-time highs. Corporate balance sheets are beach-body beautiful.

What we have is people confusing the politics of government with the economics of business. And as concerned as some people are about governments, business is good.

The predominant financial crisis for today's milking by the financial media revolves around the shape of the European economy and the 330 million citizens of the Euro zone. And those concerns are real.

Yet much less attention is given to the 3.7 billion people in the emerging markets of China, Brazil, Russia, India, Mexico, South Korea, Indonesia, and Turkey who are entering the middle class, and demanding the goods and services that we take for granted. Goods that the great companies of the world, those same great companies that are trading at dirt cheap prices, are in the business of providing.

Right now the Standard and Poors 500 index is at 1325. I'm going to come back to that number later when I get to talking about planning for retirement. But first let's talk about value. At today's prices, the price/earnings ratio for the S&P is around 7½. That's like the prettiest girl in class inviting you to prom.

The yield on US Treasuries is 1.5%. That means the earnings from stocks are 5 times the yield on bonds. Currently, the dividend yield of stocks is 60 basis points higher than what bonds are paying, with the future capital appreciation of stocks thrown in for free. Guess when the last time was that we had stocks this undervalued and bonds this overvalued? How about never, ever.

Okay, let's talk about retirement. The average age of a couple entering retirement is 62. And a lot of those people are looking back at what has happened in the stock markets and are concerned.

But let's talk not about perception, but about what really happened. Let's not talk about the earth being flat, let's talk about how things really are.

Over this couple's lifetime they have seen the Cold War, the Cuban Missile Crisis, the Kennedy Assassination, the OPEC oil crisis, runaway inflation, double digit unemployment, stagflation, soaring government deficits, the terrible recessions of the 1970s and 1980s, Black Monday, the Russian debt default, Y2K, the tech wreck, the September 11 terrorist attacks, the subprime meltdown, real estate prices crumbling, and the Great Recession.

Meanwhile, when this soon-to-be-retired couple was born, the S&P stood at a level of 17. You might recall that I told you earlier that it is currently at 1325. That's right. Despite the litany of obstacles that these guys have seen in their lifetime, the stock market is 77 times higher now.

Here's the thing. If this soon-to-be-retired couple are non-smokers, the odds are that at least one of them will live to age 92. That's a 30 year retirement in a rising-cost world that we need to plan for.

Lots of times people will tell me that they aren't going to live that long. Many of these people will be wrong. Quit thinking about your parents or grandparents life expectancy. Nowadays the statistics are for a non-smoking couple aged 62, that at least one of them will see 92. Unless your health is already compromised, failing to plan for a 30 year retirement is foolhardy.

So where was the S&P 30 years ago? I'll tell you. It was at 110. Again, today it is at 1325. From 110 to 1325 over 30 years, and that's not even factoring dividends in to the equation. Now try telling me how bad the last 30 years really was.

Taking a predominantly fixed income retirement strategy into a 30 year retirement in a rising cost world is a losing strategy. Plain and simple. All of history supports this.

And for people who are still in their accumulating years, the opportunity to acquire the great companies of the world at today's dirt cheap prices is a phenomenal opportunity. Don't let this opportunity pass you by. You might not have another like it in your lifetime.

The future is clear; it's only the timing that is uncertain.

And when it's all said and done I probably am going to say I told you so.

From July 2012

PART FOUR

Bad Things Happen to Good People Too

All your hopes and dreams are reliant on continued good health, which is inherently unreliable.

Sharp-eyed readers may notice the evolution of historical data in this section. The nuances between similar statistics are not material. The quoted statistics are merely slightly different snapshots taken at different points in time, and should not distract from the fundamental messages.

■ ■ ■ ■ ■ ■

It Will Never Happen to Me

SUNDAY, AUGUST 14 began uneventfully. It was a day that I had a few things that I wanted to get done, but nothing was pressing. It was just me in the house, so I got to sleep in a bit, a rare luxury for a parent of two small children.

After a lazy start to the day I got around to my summer project. I am building a tree fort for my kids. When it's done it should be pretty spiffy – three decks intertwined amongst a dozen or so trees; a boardwalk, a slide, tire swing, fireman's pole, monkey bars, cargo net, climbing rocks, and more. I'm certainly no carpenter, but I am really enjoying building something with my own hands that my kids should get years of enjoyment from.

So at this point I am assembling the cross braces that will support one of the decks, and I need to nail some 2 x 6s into place. From ground level I don't have a very good angle to swing the hammer, so I jump up onto the skeleton of the tree fort.

I am carefully navigating my way across the framework, examining the structure, pausing to think about what I have to do next so that everything fits together – how to attach the slide, where the cargo net will go. It's just a moment in time on a sunny Sunday afternoon, where I am working on a backyard project. Nothing out of the ordinary.

Except I am also standing on a spider web of lumber fastened to trees roughly 8 feet off the ground.

That's when I fell.

And landed on my head.

I'm 6 feet tall. So since I was standing on this lumber that was suspended roughly 8 feet off the ground, that meant my head was probably 14 feet away from Mother Earth when I lost any control of the situation that I once had. I was falling, and there was not a damn thing I could do about it.

Most readers probably haven't fallen from that height and landed on their head. And you don't want to. The physics of a 200-pound guy falling from that height generates a significant amount of force.

What happened was, as I was inching across a piece of lumber mounted on end, I had a little wobble. The wobble wasn't the problem though. The problem was that I reached out for what I thought was secure footing, and much to my surprise, found out that it was anything but. These boards were not nailed. They were barely tacked in place. I didn't step onto a firm foundation, I stepped onto the wrong end of an unsecured teeter-totter.

I was off balance, and out of control. In a split second I instinctively twisted my body towards the fall, much like a cat will. But, unfortunately, with far different results.

There was nothing I could grab for, and there was no place to leap free. I was Wile E. Coyote. Temporarily suspended in space, but plummeting to the earth is inevitable.

I went from wobble, to surprise, to inevitable in less than two seconds. But I really can't say for sure exactly what happened after that. Later, in the hospital, the doctors asked me if I lost consciousness. I think so, but I don't know how long I was out for.

All I do know is that my next conscious thought was "How bad is it?" I didn't know if my neck was broken. I didn't know if I had a wooden stake puncturing my chest. I just didn't know. But it felt bad. I've played contact sports all my life, and I've been in more than one wreck over my years, and this didn't feel like a bloody nose. This felt like 911.

A few seconds later I became a little more aware of myself and my surroundings. I realized that I had landed on a pile of timber. But my world was still pretty small. Nicole Kidman could have been suntanning on my lawn, and I wouldn't have even noticed, never mind cared. I still didn't know how bad I was hurt, but I figured I was ambulatory at least.

A few seconds after that I am able to gather myself together a bit more. There is nobody else around, I can't just lay there. If I need help I need to go get it. I reach up to check my skull, thinking that stitches are a certainty. I just didn't want to have a gaping head wound. I was fairly amazed to find bleeding, but no open lacerations.

I basically landed with a thud. Blunt trauma. To my face.

My beloved pair of Serengeti sunglasses lay in pieces under me. People who have good vision won't appreciate this. To people like me, who have needed corrective lenses their entire lives, the loss of a good pair of prescription sunglasses is cause for small mourning.

I picked up my baseball cap. Inside was a clump of my own hair. I had scalped myself.

I was missing a shoe. I still am. No idea what happened to it. Went flying into the bush, I guess.

In retrospect, judging from the various wounds to me, and the various damages to the structure of the tree fort, what appears to have happened is that I got caught up in the cross beams as I fell which may have slowed my descent, much like a skydiver falling through a canopy of tree branches, but also pin-wheeled my body so I fell head first onto the timber below.

Now the good news. I'm fine. I went and got checked out. A very sore neck, and now that the facial abrasions are starting to scab over I look like I should be in a zombie movie, but I've seen worse.

But here's the point.

I didn't wake up that day thinking I would fall head first out of a tree.

In fact, in the various stages of construction over the previous weeks, I had it occur to me many times that this is something to be careful with.

I didn't think I would fall from a tree. But I did.

The question that I want you to think about is what would happen to you, and to your family, if the unexpected happened? If there was something odd on the test results of your next physical? If that car coming through the intersection didn't see you? If your footing gave way?

In my case I was lucky. Many people won't be. Unexpected things happen. Potentially your life changes horribly in less than 2 seconds.

So what would happen if you were out of the picture? What would happen if your wife and kids were suddenly your widow and orphans?

What would happen if you were laid up in a hospital bed? Can you still pay the bills? Do you have resources that you can turn to if you can't work?

I know the answer to these questions. I am 43 years old with 2 small kids. I have $1.5 million of life insurance, $250,000 of critical illness insurance, and all the disability insurance I can buy. These are all personally owned polices. I don't rely on group or creditor insurance. Because even guys like me sometimes fall out of trees and land on their head.

What about you?

From August 2011

It's Not a Question of "If"

ONE OF THE REALITIES of my profession is that I ask people what they would like to happen when they die.

That's a question that some people don't give a lot of thought to. Not me. I think about my own death all the time. I'm not morose about it. I just think it's a damn cruel joke that, just when a guy starts to figure out a few things, his time comes to an end.

I hate it that one day I won't be here to watch over my family. It's no consolation to me that day is not likely to be here for another 50 years or so. I still hate it.

Metaphysics aside, if you have people in your life that you care about, what happens when you die is something that warrants consideration. And often this is something that gets neglected.

It's not uncommon for people to say to me, "if I die". As in, "if I die, my wife would have the insurance from work, and she'd be able to sell the house…"

There's a fundamental problem with that line of thinking, and it has nothing to do with whether your group insurance coverage is adequate, or whether your wife wants to sell the house. The problem lies in the use of the word "if".

It's not a question of "if" you die. It's a question of when.

Don't confuse the appearance of good health with immortality. In fact, don't even confuse the appearance of good health with actual good health. Not all diseases are overt, nor are all diseases easy to diagnosis. Something could be killing you insidiously right now, and you might be blissfully ignorant of it right up until its final, lethal stage. And, of course, there is always the chance of a moose coming out of a dark highway ditch right in front of your truck on an icy winter night.

All of us are going to die. We know that. The only unknown is when that last breath will be.

It seems to me that planning for something that has a 100 percent chance of happening is the wise thing to do. Further, given that death could happen at any time, to procrastinate this planning is foolhardy.

Sometimes people don't make planning for the inevitable a priority; perhaps they are under the impression when they die that things will somehow just kind of work themselves out. That's not good enough. I can tell you unequivocally that doesn't really happen, except in perhaps the very simplest of situations.

Estate planning is about arranging your affairs so that when you die the things that are important to you are addressed with a minimum of delay and expense. This goes beyond just simply making sure that your will is current, although that's a fine first step.

Simple steps may work fine for simple situations, like an all-to-wife scenario. But if you have significant assets, or a blended family, or relatives that don't always agree on things, or business partners, or you want to pay less tax, or you want to leave a legacy, or you don't want things to be tied up for longer than necessary, or you don't want to leave a mess behind for your executor to sort out, then you'll want to be proactive on this.

Let's say you own a home worth $300,000, and you have $300,000 in your RRIF, and you want the money to be split between your two adult kids. Simple, you think, I'll just leave the house to one kid, and the RRIF to the other. Only problem is, the kid who gets the house gets an asset worth 300,000. The kid who gets the RRIF doesn't get 300,000, he gets what's left of the 300,000 after taxes, and taxes might eat up around a third of the RRIF.

Or let's say that you have a family business, and one of your kids is involved in the business, but the other is not. What's the right way to distribute your assets? Splitting the business asset 50/50 between the two kids might be equal, but is it equitable? One of the kids helped make the business what it is, while the other one did not contribute. Should the kid that was active in the business see the fruits of his efforts?

Or let's say that in an effort to avoid probate fees you own an asset jointly with one of your kids. The problem is that your kid gets into financial trouble, and now his creditors are going after his portion of the jointly-held asset. Or the kid gets divorced, and now the ex-wife wants her due.

Clearly estate planning is a field where consulting with a knowledgeable professional can save a lot of time, money and aggravation. What people need to understand is that estate planning isn't just something for other people. There is a 100 percent chance that you are going to die one day. The question is, are your affairs going to be in order when that day comes?

From March 2012

Protect the Goose that Lays the Golden Eggs

I AM CURRENTLY DISABLED.

I have keratoconus, a degenerative eye disorder. As disabilities go, there are a lot of people a lot worse off than I am. At least keratoconus is treatable.

But keratoconus is no joke. 25 percent of people with keratoconus require a corneal transplant. So in September I had eye surgery and, in my post-operation recuperation, I can't see very well at all.

At the moment my vision is so bad that I had to get two feet away from my daughter Emily in order to pick her out amongst a crowd of kids, and even at that distance I had to squint to recognize my own daughter. If you saw me on the street and I didn't wave to you it's not because I'm stuck up, it's because I can't see you.

Fortunately all indications are that the surgery was successful. But what if it wasn't?

You don't really appreciate your health until you lose it. This week, as I lay on the couch, wearing sunglasses in a darkened room, listening to audio recordings of John Grisham and Ken Follett novels because I really can't do much else – I can't use the computer, can't read, can't watch TV, can't drive, can't do many things with the kids – I couldn't help but think what life would be like if my vision never returned.

Do you remember the fable of the goose that laid the golden eggs? In the story a farmer had a goose that laid an egg of pure gold every day.

Pretend for a moment that you are that farmer. As long as you have the goose you will receive a golden egg every day. With this gold you can feed your family, make your mortgage payment, cover the costs of post-secondary education for your kids, maybe even retire early and comfortably. As long as you have the goose, all this is possible.

What if you were to lose the goose? Now all of those aspirations – lifestyle, kids' education, retirement – all of it is in jeopardy.

Guess what? We are all farmers, and we all have a golden goose.

Our golden goose is our ability to earn income. For many people, their ability to earn income is their greatest asset. A 35-year-old person earning $3000 per month will earn more than $1,000,000 before age 65.

Most people discount how valuable the ability to earn income is. Further, they underestimate how fragile that ability to earn income is.

Quit kidding yourself. One out of two 25-year old people will be disabled for at least 90 days before age 65. The average duration of disability is 2.6 years.

Do you think your lifestyle reduces the risk of an accident happening to you? First thing, you can't be sure of avoiding an accident. After all, that's why they are called accidents. Second thing, illness accounts for 8 out of 10 disabilities. How can you be sure that you won't get sick?

What would happen to your finances if you had no paycheques for 2.6 years? Who would pay your mortgage, feed your family, pay your hospital bills?

Disability insurance is the answer. An iron-clad individual disability policy might run around 2.5 percent of your gross income.

Let's say I was going to hire you, and we are negotiating your contract. Contract A will pay you $60,000. However, if you can't work because you are hurt or sick I will not pay you.

Contract B will pay you $58,500. But if you are stricken with MS, or you lose your sight, or you have a heart attack, or if any of the other million things that affect your health happens, you still get paid. If this thing that happens to you occurs at age 40, I am going to pay you about $750,000 tax-free, over the next 25 years.

With the chance of disability roughly 3 times the chance of death, with disability accounting for 16 times the number of mortgage foreclosures than death, with about 40 percent of disabilities that last one year continuing for 5 or more years, the sensible option is contract B.

Many people don't hesitate to insure their stuff – their home, their car, their boat. That's like insuring the golden eggs. Just don't forget to insure the goose that provides the golden eggs. Insure yourself, and your ability to earn income.

From October 2012

■ ■ ■ ■ ■ ■

Monday Morning, 7:00 a.m.

IT'S 7:00 A.M. on a crisp, cloudless Monday in early March. The sun is just coming up, and it's going to be a beautiful day. It's that wonderful time of the morning when you have the whole day ahead of you, at that wonderful time of the year when spring is right around the corner.

My associate Meagan is walking to work, as she likes to do, and she is crossing the intersection. The red light turns green, and the walk signal is on. She's halfway through the crosswalk.

That's when the car hits her.

Meagan goes up onto the hood of the car, smacking into the windshield. She's in a daze, not understanding what just happened to her. She doesn't recall the actual moment of impact. It's not until later that the pain comes.

She's back at work now, but she needs physiotherapy three times a week. The concussion and her other injuries limit what she can do. Fortunately her work allows her to remain at her desk through the day. If she had a different profession she might still be off work. Still, her productivity (and thus, her paycheque) has been affected.

And all she was doing when this happened was walking to work. On a beautiful spring morning.

That's the thing about your health. You have it. Right up to the point when you don't.

Just about everyone takes their health for granted. But your health is fragile. Even for a 20-something vegetarian who looks after herself.

You have things you want to do in life. Retire some day. Educate your kids. Take a vacation. Maybe buy a new house. All of this depends on your ability to earn income, and your ability to earn income depends on your health.

In my line of work, I see this happen all the time. People are in the prime of their lives, and all of a sudden their health takes a dramatic turn for the worse. You can take good care of yourself, but sometimes even that is not enough.

Every year I have clients get hurt, or get sick, or pass away. These people are not merely statistics; they are your friends and neighbours.

We can do things to lessen the chances of something bad happening to us. We can (and should) eat right, exercise more, drink less and quit smoking. But that doesn't eliminate the chances of something bad happening.

So what would happen if you did get hurt or sick? Would you have enough income coming in to cover your current obligations, never mind increased medical expenses? Can you afford for your spouse to take time off work? Could you make your mortgage payment? What happens to your retirement savings? What happens to Junior's college fund?

Many people think that they have adequate coverage because they have something through work, or because they signed up for disability coverage when they took out a loan. Tragically, later on some of them find out just what is (and what isn't) covered by these type of polices. It's not at all unusual for group policies to be inadequate, and it's not at all unusual for insurance policies connected to a loan to pay limited, if any, benefits. Unfortunately, I know this because I have clients in these situations.

Many of my essays come from real life experiences. This is one of them. It started at 7:00 a.m. on a crisp, cloudless Monday in early March.

From April 2009

■ ■ ■ ■ ■ ▪

Protect Your Money

TODAY WAS A BEAUTIFUL, SUNNY FRIDAY, and we took the opportunity to do some much-needed outside maintenance. The guardrail for our wheelchair ramp is getting a new coat of paint.

As we were working away on the wheelchair ramp I realized that, in the five years that we have been in this location, we have only had one person in a wheelchair that has come see us. This person just had a few questions, I don't even know if he was in the market for our services.

As far as I know, the Chartered Accounting firm that is in my building doesn't have any clients in wheelchairs either.

As we plugged away with our sanding and painting , I came up with a theory: In general, disabled people are not looking for the services of Certified Financial Planners or Chartered Accountants.

This theory has no science at all to it, it's merely based on the anecdotal evidence that, as far as I know, the only wheelchair that has come up that ramp belonged to that fellow with the couple of questions.

Please don't get the wrong idea. We are wheelchair-friendly here. Our wheelchair ramp has a gentle slope, the doorways, hallways, and washrooms were all designed to accommodate a wheelchair.

Hey, if you have mobility concerns, you call me ahead of time, I'll come out from the back to get the door for you myself. I'm not saying that we can't take people in wheelchairs as clients; I'm saying that none of our clients are in wheelchairs.

That's not to say that disabled people never use Certified Financial Planners or Chartered Accountants, or that disabled people can't be financially successful, or whatever. Again, please don't get the wrong idea. I'm just generalizing here.

You see, the thing about it is this: statistically we should have more clients with disabilities. Modesty aside, there are a whole bunch of very smart, very qualified people that are very good at what they do that work at this address. Typically, all sorts of people seek us out. And yet, apparently not disabled people.

The point of this isn't some social commentary. In fact, I am not even writing this essay with the disabled audience in mind. Nope, this is actually for all of those able-bodied people out there.

The undeniable truth is that disabilities happen. They happen to people just like you. Indeed, they happen way more than often than you probably think.

Have you ever played the lotto? If so, you must have figured that you had a shot at winning it. In actual fact, the odds of winning the Lotto 649 draw are 1 in 13.9 million.

It's hard to get a handle on a number that big. Let me put it another way. If you bought a Lotto 649 ticket every day, seven days a week, you can expect to win the jackpot once every 38,082 years.

Meanwhile, your chance of becoming disabled for 90 days or longer at least once prior to age 65 is 1 in 3.

Again, winning the lottery: 1 in 13,900,000. Becoming disabled: 1 in 3.

Disabled people can, and do, get better. But it takes time. The average length of a disability that lasts over 90 days is 2.9 years.

So disabilities happen to a lot of people, and disabilities last for a long time. What does all this mean?

Well, ask yourself what would happen to your finances if you were suddenly hurt or sick. I'm not talking about a broken leg, which is painful, and inconvenient, but generally doesn't slow you down for too long. I mean you are seriously banged up, and you are out of action for an extended period.

What would happen to your finances? Do you have an insurance plan to replace your lost income? Is it sufficient?

Be honest with yourself, do you even know what coverage you have? If you don't know what you have then you can't know whether it is sufficient.

The truth is that most people have inadequate disability protection. Some people have group benefits, but that only goes so far. If you don't believe me take a look at what your group benefits plan actually covers.

So what happens when someone with little or no disability coverage suffers a disability? It's a simple answer. Whatever it takes.

Your savings? Gone. The line of credit? Maxed out. Retirement savings? You were hoping you could leave that alone, but what else can you do? Etcetera.

This is why I say that, in general, disabled people are not looking for the services of Certified Financial Planners or Chartered Accountants. Their disability doesn't just take their health. It takes their wealth as well.

Disabilities happen. One person in three, my friend, one person in three. When disabilities happen, your money is the second thing to go.

Talk to an insurance professional now to make sure your income protection plans are up to the task. We can't keep a disability from happening to you, but we can put you in a better financial position to deal with things that need to be dealt with.

From July 2007

What Happens When
Your Kid Gets Sick

THIS WEEK I HAD PLANNED to write about a completely different topic, until something unexpected changed everything.

My baby girl got sick.

Now when I say sick, I don't mean cancer sick. She's going to be fine.

But meanwhile she's into her 6th day of misery. She hasn't been eating much, and what she has she hasn't kept down for very long. She's lost weight, and we've had to get fluids into her with an oral syringe to keep her from getting dehydrated. We've had two trips to emergency, one to the walk-in clinic, one to our family doctor, and two to the lab for tests.

To our great relief, she's starting to show some of her usual spark. But along the way it's only natural that periodic parental fears of worst-case scenarios have crept into our minds.

Today started with one of these trips to the emergency ward. And the implication of that was that the work stuff that I had intended to tackle at 9:00 am didn't get looked at until 3:30 pm. In the big picture that's not a big deal. The kid's going to be fine, and the work eventually got done.

But the thing about it is that, finally now, after 6 days of uncertainty, it looks like Emily's illness is not something that is too serious. Concerning, sure. But not hospitalization serious.

And I still dropped everything else that was going on in my life to be with her this morning. And I would again. Without a nanosecond's hesitation. And you would too if it was your kid.

Emily's going to be fine. We know that now. But imagine if she wasn't.

What if when we went in to the emergency ward today the doctor had a different diagnosis? What if Emily didn't spend the afternoon with her Mom, napping and finally eating, but on a medivac flight to Children's Hospital? Do you think I would be sitting in my office, talking to people about their finances?

Obviously not.

Okay, Brad Brain, we're happy that your kid is alright, but what does this have to do with an essay on finances?

Everything.

Like virtually all of you, if I am not at work my personal income slows. Eventually it would stop.

So if I have a sick kid, or sick spouse, or sick parent, or any other sick loved one, and I am at their hospital bedside, and the implication (which is at the same time both initially far less important, but also eventually inescapable) is that my income is reduced, and perhaps even severed completely, how do I pay my mortgage? How do I pay my staff? How do I pay my kid's hospital bills, or the hotel and restaurant bill I'll have to be near her?

Most people recognize that insuring the income of the family breadwinner is clearly a good idea. In my own situation, if I was to be run over by a drunk driver or contracted prostate cancer or lost my eyesight our family's income would shrink by as much as 99.9%. Our bills wouldn't shrink by 99.9% though. And that's why I gladly pay the premiums on my own personal life insurance, critical illness insurance, and disability insurance premiums every year.

What I'm talking about here, though, isn't about insuring the family's income in case the breadwinner gets sick. I'm talking about insuring the family's income in case the non-income earning spouse gets sick. Or, God forbid, your kid gets sick.

Shortly after Emily was born I added a rider to my own critical illness insurance policy that would pay me a tax-free lump sum payment of $50,000 if she was diagnosed with a covered critical illness.

I did this as the new and proud parent of a wonderful, healthy and happy daughter, but also recognizing, from a purely financial perspective that our family's financial situation would be jeopardized if something were to happen to Emily.

Now that we've had our first multiple-trips-to-the-emergency-ward-for-an-as-yet-undiagnosed, but-somebody-please, please, please tell-me-what-the-hell-is-happening-to-my-daughter situation, I'm not sure that even $50,000 coverage is enough if this was the real deal.

The odds of contracting a critical illness are mind-blowing. 1 in 2 males and 1 in 3 females will have heart disease. 1 in 2.3 males and 1 in 2.6 females will develop cancer.

Terrible things don't happen only to grown men. Protect your family's finances from bad things happening. To any member of the family.

From April 2008

Insurance for Kids?

It's INTERESTING HOW some popular ideas fall out of favour, and then find resurgence. Bell-bottoms, dressing like Madonna circa 1983, and disco music are all examples. From a financial planning perspective whole life insurance is an example of an idea that fell out of favour, and is now back in style. Unlike the resurgence of disco music, however, whole life insurance is an idea that actually has some good things going for it.

Decades ago the financial planning product landscape was much simpler. Whole life insurance was a very popular product, in part because there weren't as many products to choose from.

In hindsight whole life insurance wasn't always the best fit for the applications it was used for. Additionally the product had some limitations that left it unable to adapt to a changing economic environment. Over time new products were developed, and whole life insurance was on the verge of extinction.

That was then.

We have come full circle. Nowadays when I am comparing different products I am finding that whole life insurance can be an elegant solution in the right circumstance.

Even five years ago if you told me that one day I would be writing about the merits of whole life insurance I would have gladly bet you any sum of money that it would never happen. The idea was completely contrary to the consensus opinion.

Even further, if you told me that I would even consider what I am about to tell you I wouldn't even continue the conversation. The idea seemed completely without merit. In fact, the idea was almost an affront to sensible financial planning.

I am glad that I am not completely rigid in my thinking. You see, I have looked at this from every angle, and the numbers stand up.

Are you ready for this revolutionary new (old) idea? Here it is: whole life insurance for kids. (Gasp! Say it isn't so!) Yep, whole life insurance for kids.

The critical component for this strategy to be effective is time. You aren't going to see results overnight. It's something that works, but you need to give it time to work. As in about 20 years, but really the longer the better.

Sometimes whole life policies are set up as education plans. Personally I am not big on this idea, but it can be done. I think an even better fit is when a parent or grandparent makes 18 years of contributions, and turns the policy over to Junior when the time is right, and with the intention of keeping the plan in place. It could be the only insurance policy that Junior ever needs.

I have a 40-something client whose Dad set up a policy when the client was a kid. The client considers it the best investment he has ever had. Looking at his policy, 40 years in, he is probably right.

So why does the idea work? Well, it's a combination of factors, and one of the big ingredients is the tax-efficient growth of the investment. Anytime you can grow your money without the taxman getting his grubby paws on it you have a natural advantage.

But there is a little more to why whole life is going through a renaissance, and a big part of it is the way that the investment component of a whole life policy operates. Generally speaking, a whole life policy participates in the profits of the insurance company. There are a bunch of rules that the insurance company is legally bound to follow. At the end of the day it comes down to prudent, fiscally responsible management. How prudent? Well, how about never, ever having a negative return on your money. That kind of prudent.

Not everyone wants to look at their kid's investment/insurance statements every day. And that's what you get with whole life. A low maintenance, sleep-at-night, long-term idea that gives your kids an 18-year head start. I like it.

Do yourself a favour and get a quote or two. It took me a while to come around, and it's still not a solution for every situation, but like I say, in the right circumstance, the numbers stand up.

From March 2004

You Survive, But Do Your Finances?

THIS TOPIC IS important. Don't just quickly skim over this one.

Critical illness. It is a reality that you need to face.

The problem:1 in 2 men and 1 in 3 women will develop heart disease in their lifetime, according to the Heart and Stroke Foundation. According to the National Cancer Institute of Canada, 1 in 2.5 men and 1 in 2.8 women will develop cancer. Scary statistics.

With the amazing advances in medicine, critical illness does not kill people like it used to. According to the Heart and Stroke Foundation, 85 percent of hospitalized heart attack patients survive. 75 percent of stroke patients survive the initial event.

So if people are not dying like they used to, what's the problem? The problem is money. Let's say I develop a cancer. And it's pretty bad.

Where is my income going to come from? Who is going to pay for my medical treatment? What if my home needs renovations to accommodate a wheelchair? What if I can get treatment quicker if I can get down to the USA?

I already have lots of life insurance. But what good will that do me if I am not dead yet?

A critical illness can play havoc with a person's finances. Treatment can be expensive and time off from work can compound the problem.

The solution: critical illness insurance.Critical illness insurance pays a tax-free lump-sum benefit to you on the diagnosis and survival of a covered critical illness.

Sometimes people see the need for critical illness insurance, and other times they hesitate. After all, the premium has to be paid. What if a person doesn't get sick?

That's a fair question. And I have an elegant answer. It's called a return-of-premium rider.

In simple terms, the return-of-premium rider means that if you don't use the policy then you get your money back. Is this cool, or what? If you get sick, then you have a policy that will pay you a tax-free benefit just at a time when the money is going to come in pretty handy. But if you don't get sick you get your money back.

There are some different policies out there, and they have different features, so it pays to shop the market. Some, for instance, only offer partial return of premium while others offer a full return of premium.

Critical Illness Insurance is not life insurance, and it is not disability insurance. Life insurance pays if you die, critical illness insurance pays if you get sick, but live. Disability insurance pays if your income is reduced. Critical Illness Insurance is not tied to income.

You still face the same risk or heart attack, stroke or cancer whether or not you have a critical illness insurance policy. It's just that having the policy will transfer the financial risk from you to an insurance company.

There are no ideal alternatives to a Critical Illness Insurance policy. Critical Illness Insurance will pay a tax-free lump sum benefit if you are diagnosed with and survive a covered critical illness. That can allow you to focus on what's most important ... getting better.

From July 2005

PART FIVE

What Do You Think the Odds Are that You Will Get There Purely by Chance?

If you don't know where you are going,
then any road will do.

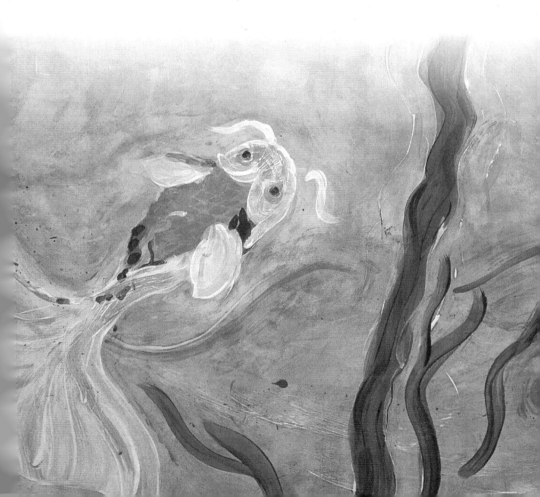

What's Important About Money to You?

THIS IS ONE OF THOSE philosophical essays intended to make a person stop to consider about what is important.

Many times people think about money in the sense of it allows them to buy a quad or a boat. Obviously, accumulating wealth allows us to buy things that give us gratification. And that's important.

Personally, I just spent another ridiculous amount of money on my motorcycle this winter. My bike wasn't running well at the end of the summer, and so it has been in the shop over the winter months. Last month I got a call from the Harley dealership, and they found that I had a blown head gasket, and since they were going to be working on the engine anyway, did I want them to port and polish the heads while they were at it?

Logically this made no sense. The upgrades cost me an extra $2000 for them to make my bike go faster. That's more than I paid for my first motorcycle, and the thing about it is the bike goes fast enough as it is. I probably won't even notice the difference in performance unless I am seriously breaking the speed limit, and that's not the way I ride.

But I love to ride, and I love the performance of the machine, and to be honest, I don't mind the bragging rights when I'm talking bikes with the boys. Riding my motorcycle puts a smile on my face, so I spent the money.

But this isn't about quads and boats and bikes, although these things are good because they give us pleasure. It's important to have balance between the things that give us pleasure, and the great goals in life. This is about the great goals in life.

Money is more about the ability to accumulate stuff. Money also gives us the freedom to live life the way we want – to do the things we want to do, and to be the people we want to be.

Here's a question: what is important about money to you? Think about it for a minute, it's an important question.

But the next question is even more important, because it reveals a bit about your values: What's important about the answer to the question "What's important about money to you?"

In other words, let's say that I was to ask, "What's important about money to you?" and you said, "I would like to retire comfortably." The follow up question is, "What's important about retiring comfortably to you?" The answer to this might be "It would allow me to spend more time with family," or "I would be able to spend more time working with my favourite charity." The answers to these types of questions are the ones that lead to your own personal great goals in life, and money is the vehicle that allows you to reach those personal great goals.

I heard a great expression the other day, "Money Jail". Money Jail keeps you from reaching the great goals in life. There are some different ways that you can end up in Money Jail.

You might end up in Money Jail because of being so focused on accumulating stuff like quads and boats and bikes that you don't have anything left for the things that are really important to you.

You might end up in Money Jail because you are so fearful of running out of money that you never pursue your great goals. As odd as it sounds, some people who are in a virtually impervious financial position don't live the life of their dreams.

Your ego could land you in Money Jail. Many people compare themselves to others and they try to keep up with what they perceive as being expectations, or they rationalize that they deserve luxury items that they really can't afford.

Wealth is not really about how much money you have. Wealth is a state of mind. Wealth is relative, not absolute. Many people with smaller bank balances are truly wealthy people. On the other hand, there are millionaires that are not wealthy.

What brings you peace? What have you been saying that you always wanted to do with your life, if only you had the time and the money? These are the great goals in life, and are truly worth working towards.

What is important about money to you?

From March 2006

The Essence of Buffett

SOMETIMES I WILL MEET A PERSON in a casual setting, maybe a backyard barbeque, and the conversation turns to my work. The stock market has a certain allure about it. Sometimes the person has some questions about what I would consider to be a hot investment. Some people might expect that I have some inside information or particular insight about a stock that is about to bust loose.

It's true that does happen. And some people can make money on a hot stock idea. It's just that I don't choose to be part of that lunacy.

That's not to say that I don't believe in equity investing. I believe in it whole-heartedly. I just don't buy into the Wall Street marketing that a person should buy a stock now because it is about to take off.

The thing to remember is that the stock market is an auction process. And there is a dirty little cycle that happens in which an investor buys a stock because it is moving up, and then the increased demand for the stock drives the price up further, which gets more investors interested, which drives the price up further, and so it goes.

There are all sorts of theories on how to profit from this phenomenon; momentum investing, sector rotating, and market timing are all examples. Personally I think those are lousy investment strategies. After all, sooner or later the music is going to stop and when it does there won't be enough chairs for all of the practitioners of these hare-brained strategies.

So what do I believe in? I believe in buying businesses, not buying stock. There is a big, big, big difference.

A very wise person once said that if you want to be successful the way to do it is to find the leading authority in the field, and copy his recipe for success exactly. Not your version of his recipe, mind you. If a world-class chef gave you his recipe for lobster thermidor you don't take the recipe home and experiment with adding cayenne pepper if you are looking to duplicate the results of the world-class chef.

So if we are looking for superior investment results that come from buying wonderful businesses the superstars upon which we should model our own behavior are Ben Graham and Warren Buffett. This, I feel, is both self-evident and indisputable.

Here is the essence of the investing philosophy of Ben Graham and Warren Buffett.

First, pay no attention to all the fancy theories and stratagems dreamed up by economists and journalists. For instance, the efficient market hypothesis says that stocks always trade at their correct value because all information that is needed to make a decision about buying a stock is readily available and easily disseminated. The efficient market hypothesis sounds great in a textbook, but from a practical point of view it has limited application and, even worse, little empirical evidence that it is valid. Did Nortel trade at the correct price four years ago when it was sky high? Does it trade at the correct price today now that the share price has been obliterated?

Rather, look at a company as a business. The purpose of investing is to earn a rate of return on your money. So how much money does the business generate? Do the earnings of the business adequately compensate you for your invested capital?

The intrinsic value of a company is the net present value of the earnings of a business from now until the end of the world. It might be an exciting company with a bright future, but from an investment point of view that doesn't mean that we want to pay more for it than the business is worth.

Invest with a margin of safety. Having determined the intrinsic value of a business we want to pay something less than that to acquire the business. The idea is that we want to buy a dollar for 60 cents. Or 50 cents. Or 30 cents. The bigger the margin of safety, the less the chance of the investment going sour.

Invest in what you know. Knowledge is the one true way to protect your capital. If you don't know enough not only about the company, but also its competitors and the industry itself, then why would you stake your hard-earned money on it?

There is no quota for the number of investments that you must make. Nobody forces investments down your throat. So wait for the can't-miss, slam-dunk, no-brainer opportunities. Buffett likens it to a baseball game in which there are no called strikes. You can sit at the plate and wait and wait until finally that one perfect pitch comes.

Take big positions when the opportunity presents itself. If you truly understand the business, and you can buy it at a discount to its intrinsic value and with an attractive margin of safety, then it's time to back up the truck and load up. Only meaningful positions generate meaningful results. If you have 100 positions in a portfolio, and one of them doubles in value, the impact on your portfolio as a whole will be negligible simply because your exposure is limited.

Watch the playing field, not the scoreboard. What happens on the field determines the results. The playing field is where the business operates. The scoreboard is the price of the stock. Remember which is which.

The stock market is your servant, not your master. Graham describes a peculiar fellow named Mr. Market who faithfully shows up each morning and offers to buy securities from you or to sell securities to you. The thing about Mr. Market is he is manic-depressive. Sometimes he shows up and is absolutely euphoric about a security, and is willing to buy it from you at an inflated price. Other days he shows up and is completely despondent about a security, and is willing to sell it to you at a ridiculously low price. You can choose to enter into a transaction with him, or to ignore him altogether. In either case he will show up again tomorrow.

Exercise patience and discipline. At the recent Berkshire Hathaway Annual Inc. General Meeting Buffett attributed his success to discipline. He stays within his circle of competence. He isn't tempted to deviate from the recipe. He didn't add any cayenne pepper to Graham's recipe, and we shouldn't add cayenne to his.

From May 2004

■ ■ ■ ■ ■ ■

Profiting from the Follies of Mr. Market

RECENTLY, IN THE MIDDLE of a day when the markets ended up nearly three percent, my associate Meagan asks me if I happened to catch the day's market action. I say, "Yeah, it's too bad that most people won't get their confidence back until the markets are up 20 percent."

The markets are down right now. This is the time that long-term investors should be thinking about buying quality investments. Many won't be though. Many people won't have much confidence right now.

A good number of these people won't get their confidence back until the markets "show some stability." That's another way of saying until the markets recover lost ground. What this really means is that many investors won't get back into the markets until they are up by another 20 percent or so; missing out on a nice chunk of the recovery.

The fact that many people will spend the first part of the recovery on the sideline speaks more to human nature than it does to the economic circumstances of the day. It's not that this is the first recession we've had to deal with. Far from it. It's not that this behavior is new either. It happens every time the markets get a little hairy.

The other day I picked up a book that a friend gave me back in 1991, another recessionary time. That recession is a distant memory now, but back in the day it was topical enough that David Letterman had the "Top Ten Government Euphemisms for a Recession" for one of those top ten lists that he does. (Number one on the list – "It's Krazy Dollar Days".)

The 1991 recession saw unemployment at roughly twice the level that it is now. Back then, just as progress was finally being made on getting inflation under control, the economic slowdown necessitated the lowering of interest rates, sparking fears of a return to the bad-old days of the double-digit inflation that we saw in the 1970s and the 1980s. There were plenty of things to worry about in 1991, and many investors headed for the sidelines. In hindsight, what they really did was miss the start of one of the greatest decades ever for economic growth.

Now 1991 is a faded memory, but the pattern remains. Things get hairy, people try to sit it out on the sideline, and end up missing the good growth that happens at the start of the recovery.

This is because many people have never been introduced to Mr. Market.

Ben Graham introduced the world to "Mr. Market" in the classic 1949 investing text "The Intelligent Investor." Mr. Market is a metaphor for how people should look at investments.

Every day Mr. Market shows up and offers to both sell securities to you, and to buy securities from you. Mr. Market has a personality trait that is very important to keep in mind when considering his offers; Mr. Market is obliging, but he is also manic-depressive. Sometimes his offers are reasonable, and sometimes his offers are ridiculous.

Investors are free to accept Mr. Market's offers to buy or sell securities, or they can just simply ignore him. Regardless of what you think of Mr. Market's offers, he'll show up again tomorrow to make new offers.

You might own a security that is relatively stable, nicely profitable, and has reasonable prospects for the future. Emotions aside, this security will have a fair market value. But Mr. Market is a very moody fellow. "Emotions aside" is not an expression that he is familiar with.

The security remains relatively stable, nicely profitable, and has reasonable prospects for the future, but Mr. Market is sometimes so euphoric about this security that he will offer to buy yours at highly inflated prices, far above the fair market value. On the other hand, sometimes he'll be so despondent that he will be willing to sell this very same security at fire sale prices, far below fair market value. Although it is the exact same security – relatively stable, nicely profitable, and has reasonable prospects for the future, Mr. Market's moods are extraordinarily fickle.

The point of Graham's metaphor is the investor is best to concentrate on the intrinsic value of the security, rather than being swayed by Mr. Market's irrational and highly volatile mood swings. This allows a person to profit from Mr. Market's folly, rather than participating in it. When Mr. Market offers a deal that makes good sense, you can take him up on his offer. When he offers a deal that doesn't make sense, you can just walk away.

If Mr. Market's passionate opinions sway you, you may find yourself agreeing with him. He might persuade you to come around to his way of thinking about things.

When he's excited about the prospects for a security, you might also find yourself getting excited, and end up agreeing with his overinflated estimation of the security's true worth. These are the people that bought Nortel in 2000 and paid as much as $1245 per share for it. Today Nortel is looking at bankruptcy.

Conversely, sometimes a person might find themselves agreeing with Mr. Market's terrifying pessimism, and find themselves talked out of the opportunity that comes when quality securities trade at fire sale prices. And that's what some people are doing right now.

Mr. Market is mighty glum at the moment. And for some people, a good many people actually, it's easier to follow the crowd than it is to focus on the fundamentals; what securities are really worth, and what they are trading at today. These are the people who are going to sit on the sidelines until they realize that Mr. Market's moods have shifted again, and these securities are trading 20 percent higher than they are today.

But you don't have to be dictated to by Mr. Market's manic-depressive rants. Mr. Market is there to serve you, not to lead you. You can profit from Mr. Market's follies, and you don't have to participate in them.

From February 2009

■ ■ ■ ■ ■ ■

The Stock Market Is Like
Riding a Motorcycle

Two of my favourite things are investments and motorcycles. The other day I realized that the stock market and riding a motorcycle have something in common.

In order to turn a corner at speed on a motorcycle you need to counter-steer. Counter-steering is a pretty weird idea when a person is learning how to ride a motorcycle. It is the exact opposite of what you might expect needs to be done.

Think of riding a bicycle. If you want to turn right, you steer around a corner by turning the handlebars to the right. The right handlebar will come towards your body.

Riding a motorcycle requires the opposite actions. At speeds over 20 kilometers per hour centrifugal force takes over and the motorcycle acts like a big gyroscope. What this means is that in order to turn right you will actually push the right handlebar away from yourself. To turn left you must push the left handlebar away. Push right, go right. Push left, go left.

Riding a motorcycle requires action that is opposite from what initially seems natural. Similarly, being an investor in the stock market can require action that is opposite to a person's initial natural reaction.

Two of the most common mistakes that investors make are to buy high and to sell low. The funny thing about this is that some people recognize the folly of these investment traps, and yet rush in to do it anyway.

Let's take the first mistake, buying high. Making money is a very tough thing to do to if you buy high. Unfortunately, it happens all the time. Let's say your buddy tells you about a stock that has just zoomed up. Often people react to this news by wanting to buy some for themselves.

It is true that one possible outcome is the investment will continue to appreciate. However, the simple and undeniable truth is that if the investment has already soared, it probably will dip sooner or later. It doesn't matter how much money your buddy made, or how smart he is, or how much time he spends researching investments. Investments that grow by seventy or eighty per cent per year do not do so indefinitely.

Let's take the second mistake, selling low. Investing requires patience. There have been lots of times that a person's mutual fund has declined immediately after a purchase. Usually people realize that this can happen, and just leave things as is.

Sometimes, however, a person will see an investment go down, and they will panic. They may think to themselves, "Ouch, I just lost ten percent, I better get out before it's too late." What they have just done is crystallized their loss by selling low.

Sometimes it does make sense to get out of an investment, but that's not what I am talking about here. There are legitimate reasons to cut your losses, but I am talking about the commonplace mistake of a person with a long time frame selling a high-quality portfolio because of some temporary market volatility.

A person makes money by buying low and selling high. However, it is a natural reaction to do the opposite – to buy high and to sell low. Just like counter-steering a motorcycle a true investor will do the opposite of the natural initial reaction.

When markets are down, don't sell. Look to pick up some wonderful investments at bargain prices. When markets are high, don't buy an investment at an inflated price. There are plenty of opportunities out there, and it is not necessary to pay expensive prices for average companies.

In the end it's pretty simple. If you buy high and sell low you lose money. To maximize your chances of a successful investing outcome you must avoid both parts. Don't buy an investment that has recently experienced unsustainable levels of growth. Don't jettison an investment because it is temporarily out of favour.

From August 2000

■ ■ ■ ■ ■ ■

The Five Ages of Can't

I RARELY DECLINE AN INVITATION to speak to a group of high school students, and I always tell them about the power of compound interest. To make a point, I might use an example of a twenty-year old investing just $100 per month at 12 percent, and retiring at age 65 with $1.7 million.

Unfortunately, many people don't learn this lesson until later in life. Or rather, they know that they should be putting some money away; they just choose to not do much about it.

In the real world, many people wait until the right time in their lives to start investing. I understand this phenomenon completely. Let's face it; there are a lot of things that you want to do and that you need to do, and these things cost money. It's quite easy to justify a decision to delay squirreling a little money away.

I understand this phenomenon, I just don't agree with it.

Waiting for the right time in your life to invest often means that your life goes like this. This is called the Five Ages of Can't.

Up until age 30 you might say to yourself, "I can't save now. I'm just getting started in life. I don't make a lot yet and I'm entitled to a little fun when I'm young. There is plenty of time. Wait until I start making a little more. Then I'll save."

Then you hit the next stage in your life. From age 31 to 45 you might say, "I can't save now. I've got a growing family on my hands. Children and a house cost a lot of money. It takes all I have just to keep them going. As soon as they are a little older, it'll cost less. Then I'll save."

A little more time passes. Between age 46 and 55 you might find yourself saying, "I can't save now. I've got two children in college. It's all I can do to pay their expenses. In fact, I had to borrow for their tuition last fall. This is the most expensive period of a person's life. I can't save a penny."

Now you are in your pre-retirement years. But that doesn't mean that things get any easier. You might find yourself between ages 56 and 65, saying, "I can't save now. I know I should. But I can't seem to catch a break. It's not easy for a person my age to step out and get a better job. I'll have to ride along where I am. Maybe I'll catch a break."

So now you are age 65, and you are entering what is supposed to be your golden years. You've lived your life, and you've had some good times, but along the way you never really found that right time to put some money away. Unfortunately, now you could be saying, "I can't save now. We're living with my son and his wife. My Canada Pension does not go far. I wish I had started saving 20 years ago, but it's too late now. You can't save when there is no income."

The truth is that it's never a "good" time to save some money. There is always something else that seems to be a priority.

And yet it's always a good time to save some money.

Your life is going to happen, whether you are ready for it or not. One day you will turn 65. Whether you are ready for it, or not.

Retirement is closer than you think. You have choices that you can make. You can choose to put yourself squarely in the 5 Ages of Can't, and choose to wait for the right time to start saving some money.

Or you can choose to get going. It's up to you.

From May 2007

Don't Touch It

I JUST CAUGHT UP with a young fellow that I set up with some investments back in 2000. He was a student at the time, and he has moved around a bit in the years between then and now, so it's been harder to get a hold of him over the years.

The reason that I mention this is that, although we periodically did some minor account maintenance on his mutual funds, for the most part his investments have remained untouched for the last seven years.

The guy's Retirement Savings Plans have had an annualized return of 10.7 percent since 2000. His non-registered account has done even better, yielding an annualized return of 11.21 percent. These are decent performance numbers, but they are even more impressive given the very challenging market conditions that we saw from 2000 to 2003.

Now here's the thing. Along the way many people, even myself at times, would have considered the investments that he owns to be less than attractive. There certainly would have been the temptation to fiddle with the portfolio along the way.

And if I could have gotten a hold of him through the years I can't say for sure that we wouldn't have made some moves, maybe even moves that wouldn't have turned out as well as the stuff that we initially set up.

As it turns out, at one point one of his investments had the notoriety of being named the worst mutual fund in the country. That's saying something. To be the very worst out of thousands of competitors is not an easy task to accomplish.

The pundits have scarcely been much kinder to his other holdings either. Two of his funds are widely despised, and have suffered extended periods of investor redemptions.

A fourth fund has been so bad at times that I am actually a little surprised that the sponsoring company hasn't found a reason to bury it by consolidating it into a fund with a similar mandate. His fifth and final holding hasn't done much since 2001 either.

So there you have it. Five dogs. If I were to meet with the fellow for the first time today not one of the funds that he owns is on my short list of products that I utilize. And I wouldn't use all five of them for this size of account. But that's now, and this was then.

Well, that's all fine and good, but then how does one explain how this fellow ended up with double-digit returns from out-of-favour investments through one of the worst bear markets in modern history?

Simple. We didn't touch the portfolio along the way.

Somewhere along the way I heard a great analogy that has stuck with me. Your investment is like a bar of soap. The more you touch it, the smaller it gets.

You know, it's funny. There are lots of people who invest for the long term, and yet they check their account statement all the time. Some of them check it every day.

Many of these "investors" get their knickers in a twist if their investment has a bad year, or a bad quarter, or a bad month, or even a bad week. And they are tempted to make changes.

It's quite common that these changes don't work out. A fellow named David Dreman expressed this when he said, "How quickly investors flock to better-performing mutual funds, even though financial researchers have shown that the 'hot' funds in one time period very often turn out to be the poorest performers in another."

Why do people want to try to change horses in the middle of a race? A lot of it has to do with the constant micro-analysis that the media subjects on investment funds. A lot of it has to do with how frequently an investor looks at his long-term investment.

People, it's supposed to be long-term. Don't touch it.

Imagine if the assessed value of your house appeared in the local newspaper every day for all to see. Would you sell it if the assessed value declined one day? Of course not. Real estate is usually a long-term investment. So why would it be different with your investment funds?

By the way, for those of you who think that real estate doesn't fluctuate, you probably don't remember the 1990's – a decade of stagnant Canadian real estate prices – even in Vancouver, the hottest real estate market in the country. Famed Canadian economist John Kenneth Galbraith once said, "Genius is a short memory in a bull market."

One more quote for you. The legendary Ben Graham said, "An investor's worst enemy is not the stock market but one's self."

Your investment is like a bar of soap. The more you touch it the smaller it gets. So don't touch it.

From May 2007

Rain Makes Rainbows

SOME PUNDITS ARE PREDICTING a sharp and nasty sell-off in the markets. I hope it happens. I really do.

Hysteria? Panic? Bring it on!

No, I am not masochistic. The reason that I want a little market volatility from time to time is because volatility creates opportunity. In fact, you need some volatility from time to time in order to get above-average returns on your investments.

But wait a moment. What about the U.S. trade and budget deficits? What about currency? What about the collapsing U.S. housing market? What about the sub-prime crisis, and the chaos on the U.S. debt markets?

Well, what about it?

Frequent readers of these essays are well aware that Warren Buffett is a person that I hold in the highest regard. Amongst other things, he is the World's Greatest Investor. Buffett says, "Be greedy when others are fearful, and fearful when others are greedy."

What does that mean? Well, right now there are some companies that are in rough shape, and they are trading at cheap prices. Here's something important – I don't care. I don't care about these companies, or what price they are trading at because I'm simply not interested in companies that are in rough shape.

Now, with this big, dark cloud of uncertainty hanging over us, there are also some companies in fine shape that are also trading at a cheaper price. We have had solid companies with bright futures, in strong industries, run by great people, and they have come down in price too.

This is not unusual. When there is a pervasive cloud of doom and gloom the markets rarely discriminate between good companies and bad ones. When the tide goes out all boats float a little lower.

Here's the other important part: this, on the other hand, is something that I am very much interested in. When good companies are available at good prices, good investment returns generally follow.

This advice, which is basically nothing more complicated than the "buy low" part of "buy low, sell high", can be hard to follow. Intuitively it makes sense, but the reality is that most people are not hard-wired like Buffett.

I have a theory on why people recognize the truth of what I say, and yet are slow to act. Most people actually have two comfort zones when it comes to investing.

The first comfort zone is the paper comfort zone. This reflects how comfortable they are with the concept of volatility when they are sitting in my office, warm and dry and sipping coffee, and the idea of the markets going down by 20 percent is merely a hypothetical.

Then there is the trial-by-fire comfort zone. How people actually react when the markets really do experience a period of volatility can often differ from how they say they will react when the idea is still a hypothetical.

I know that volatility can be hard to deal with, and often it requires a leap of faith. But if you want to talk about a leap of faith, let me tell you about the first time I went skydiving!

I was having a hard time figuring out how I was going to step out the open door of an airplane and have just a postage-stamp size piece of canvas attached to this ramshackle little harness with cord no bigger than sewing thread (or so it seemed at the time) get my 210 pound frame safely back to earth.

I knew the theory behind skydiving. I knew the instructors had safely parachuted hundreds of times themselves. I knew that the equipment was thoroughly checked out beforehand. Heck, I even saw that tiny young lady do it right in front of me, and she seemed to be floating down safely.

But, even knowing all that, it was a leap of faith to step out the open door of an airplane at 3000 feet.

Sometimes investing can take a leap of faith. But, just like the skydiving instructor, I'm here to tell you it's going to be okay.

With a well-diversified portfolio you can ride out a rough patch. And you certainly need to distinguish between the good companies and the ones that aren't. But given all that, remember that time in the office, sitting warm and dry and drinking coffee, when you agreed that "buy low" was a good idea? If you believe in "buy low, sell high", now is the time to start thinking about buying.

Here's another famous Buffett quote, and it comes in the form of a short quiz: "If you plan to eat hamburgers throughout your life and are not a cattle producer, should you wish for higher or lower prices for beef? Likewise, if you are going to buy a car from time to time but are not an auto manufacturer, should you prefer higher or lower car prices? These questions, of course, answer themselves. "

"But now for the final exam: If you expect to be a net saver during the next five years, should you hope for a higher or lower stock market during that period?"

"Many investors get this one wrong. Even though they are going to be net buyers of stocks for many years to come, they are elated when stock prices rise and depressed when they fall. In effect, they rejoice because prices have risen for the "hamburgers" they will soon be buying."

"This reaction makes no sense. Only those who will be sellers of equities in the near future should be happy at seeing stocks rise. Prospective purchasers should much prefer sinking prices."

Volatility creates opportunity, and you need the rain in order to have the rainbow. If you believe in "buy low, sell high", now is the time to start thinking about buying.

From August 2007

■ ■ ■ ■ ■ ■

Keeping Your Cool When the Markets Don't

STOCK MARKETS AROUND THE WORLD have been nasty for about a year now. With part of the reason behind the recent turmoil being the rapid rise in the price of energy, this has some pundits drawing comparisons to the bad times that we saw in the markets following the oil shocks of the 1970s.

From January 1, 1973 to October 3, 1974 a hypothetical Canadian dollar investment in the Standard & Poors 500 Index would have declined by 44%, turning a $10,000 investment into $5,562.

So are we seeing the same thing all over again? Well, probably not exactly the same thing. But here's hoping.

Yep, that's right. I'd love to see a repeat of the 1970s. Savvy investors made a lot of money after investments became that cheap to own.

Of course, how a person fares in times of market turmoil all depends on what they do about it.

Many people are tempted to sell their shares and get out of the market when things get rough. That's certainly an option. Others will bite their lip and ride out the rough patch. Savvy investors, though, will take advantage of cheap prices and put some more money to work.

The good folks at Trimark have done some back-testing to see how these different ideas played out using the historical data.

One of the things that you could do would be to sell your shares and invest the proceeds in a Guaranteed Investment Certificate. GICs are nice and steady. Of course, they don't pay very much, but they don't fluctuate.

If you had sold your shares at the bottom of the market in 1974 it would have taken 6.08 years for you to regain your $10,000. By December 31, 2007 your $10,000 would have grown to $76,450.

When things get rough some people head for the exits, thinking that they will get back in once things look a little better.

If you had sold your shares, waited a year for things to stabilize, and then got back in the markets, you would have recouped your $10,000 in 5.25 years. Your $10,000 would grow to $258,680 by December 31, 2007.

Some people react to the market volatility by doing nothing. This is actually a perfectly acceptable option. It's the first idea that we have looked at so far that doesn't involve buying high and selling low.

If you had held your shares and rode things out, it would have taken 2 years for your investment to recover. By December 31, 2007 your $10,000 investment would be worth $379,462.

Now, I've already mentioned that savvy investors will look beyond short-term market volatility to the potential long-term gains that come from buying quality investments at distressed prices.

What if a person had put another $1500 into the markets after they had dropped? This is where things get interesting. Now it takes just 1.33 years to make up that lost ground, and the $11,500 total investment grows to an impressive $481,970 December 31, 2007.

Dollar cost averaging is a great way to make volatility your friend. History bears that out here. If a person had added $1000 per year to their investment over the next 10 years, they would have recouped their investment in 1.33 years, and by December 31, 2007 they have a nice little nest egg of $696,128 from the $20,000 that they invested.

Most impressive of all – consider what would have happened if a person viewed the 44% decline not with trepidation, but as the opportunity that it was, and invested a second $10,000. They would have made their money back in a scant 0.42 years, and that $20,000 investment would grow to $1,061,649 by December 31, 2007.

The moral of the story? It took investors who remained committed to their long-term goals significantly less time to recover from a rather nasty 44% decline in their investments, and those investments would now be worth significantly more than those who fled for something "safer."

The markets are down right now. The question is, what are you going to do about it?

Is this current volatility a repeat of the 1970s? I sure hope so.

From September 2008

■ ■ ■ ■ ■ ■

Victim or Opportunist

SEPTEMBER 2008 WAS AN INTERESTING MONTH. Markets around the world continued to show above-average volatility, including two separate days of daily declines of more than six percent for the Toronto Stock Exchange.

I've heard more than a few comments this month along the lines of "you must be busy." Which is absolutely true. September was our busiest month since the retirement savings plan season. Maybe even our busiest month of the year.

But it hasn't been busy around here for the reason that these people think. Although we have had our share of conversations with people who are apprehensive about the current market conditions, we've probably had three people who are looking to take advantage of the current opportunities for everyone who needs a little reassurance that everything is going to turn out okay.

This is not a common situation across the country. September saw a significant number of Canadian investors redeem their accounts, with almost $5 billion pulled out of mutual funds in Canada last month. I could be wrong, but don't recall a single one of our clients redeeming their account in September.

You see, a person has a choice when confronted with adversity in the investment markets. They can be a victim. Or they can be an opportunist.

Warren Buffett put $8 billion to work this past week alone, with options for another $8 billion. And he's 78.

Now obviously everybody's situation is unique, and not everyone will be in a position to invest money after the markets come down significantly. But if you don't want to buy when the markets are down, just exactly when were you thinking about doing some investing? After the market go back up?

As a matter of fact, that's what most people will do here. The $5 billion that came out of the markets across Canada in September will likely go back into the markets after things go back up. That's just the way that the average guy on the street thinks. Things go down, so people panic and sell. After things go back up they get a little confidence back, and buy back in at higher prices.

A different approach, the one favoured by savvy investors, is to take advantage of price weakness and to buy more at cheap prices. That's what Buffett just did.

The thing that I want to emphasize is this doesn't mean that a person would want to blindly buy purely because something has come down in price. There are outfits out there that were trading at $18 that are now trading at 8 cents. There is a reason for that. No need to throw good money after bad.

But there are also wonderful companies that were trading at $44 that are now trading at $36. A person could look at that and say, "Geez, I'm down 20 percent. I'm going to get out while I can." Or they can say, "20 percent cheaper? Get me some more!"

I relish opportunities like this. Today I had met with a fellow who has a long time frame for his investments, and a three year return of negative nine percent. Other people might be put off by that. Not me. We went through his portfolio, and he doesn't own anything that is permanently impaired by recent market developments. Its good stuff that is appropriate for him and it's now cheaper to buy than it was before.

He's not put off either. He's topping up his retirement savings plan right now, while high quality investments are cheap to buy.

Will they get cheaper yet? Maybe. We don't sweat that.

One of Buffett's very lucrative investments happened decades ago when he bought shares in The Washington Post. At the time these shares were trading at less than the liquidation value of the company, with no consideration whatsoever given to the substantial value of the company as a going concern. In other words, you could have just sold off the assets of the company and made a nice profit on your investment,

As Buffett tells the story, you could be in a life raft in the middle of the Atlantic Ocean at midnight, and people would have rowed out to find you so that they could buy the different parts of the company. The assets were that valuable, and the company was that cheap to buy.

But most people weren't buying. They thought the shares would get even cheaper yet. And they did get cheaper after Buffett bought into the company, as a matter of fact. But the $11 million that he spent to buy the company was valued at $1.3 billion in the last Berkshire Hathaway annual report.

Which brings us back to here and now. There is significant market volatility right now. We can't change that. What we can do, though, is decide how you are going to handle it.

Are you a victim of this market volatility? Or an opportunist?

From October 2008

This Time Is Not Different

THE FOUR MOST DANGEROUS WORDS in investing are "This time it's different."

Well, actually this time it's not different. It never is.

So why is there so much volatility in the stock market these days? Well, I can sum it up in one word. Panic.

But why are people panicking? Now, that is an interesting question.

To understand what is going on right now, you need to understand that there is a difference between the economy and the stock market. The economy is the collective sum of all the business activity in the country. The stock market is the collective sum of what people perceive these businesses to be worth. The economy and the stock market are not at all the same thing.

The Canadian economy, believe it or not, is just fine, thank you very much. Unemployment is at a 30 year low. Sure, we've got issues in the forestry and manufacturing sectors. That doesn't change the fact that, not only is unemployment at a thirty year low, but Canada just added another 100,000 jobs.

As of the most recent data available, the Gross Domestic Product was still growing. Sure, it is not growing as fast as it was before. Regardless, as of the most recent data available, the fact remains that the Canadian economy is growing.

Canadian banks are considered to be the safest in the world. Let me repeat. The international community considers Canadian banks to be the safest in the world.

These things are not my opinion. These things are the way it is. The Canadian economy is fine. It is people's perceptions that are causing the turbulence.

Now here's the thing that you need to know. In the long run, share prices always follow the business profits. They have to. And, again, the Canadian economy is fine.

So how come when I turn on my television I see six consecutive stories about how bad it is out there?

That's an easy question to answer, actually. Bad news makes for good stories. Good stories get your attention. Getting your attention is how the media sells their advertising. In other words, bad news sells.

Tonight we were watching Animal Planet on TV, and the program featured a major metropolitan zoo. I'm sure that when the camera crew went to the zoo that day they shot miles of footage. They could have run stories about the happy kids who got to see the animals, or the successful wildlife conservation programs. They could have talked about the habitat of the Striped Skunk. Heck, they could have talked about the logistics of the sewer system that accommodates millions of visitors a year.

But they didn't focus on that stuff. They focused on a tiger cub that had to be euthanized shortly after birth. This tiny little cub, all helpless and cute, bundled up in a towel, didn't look any bigger than a kitten, had to be put down because when Momma tiger bit through the umbilical cord, she also severed the cub's hind leg.

With all the stories that the TV program could have run, why did the tiger cub story get the attention? Well, very simply, the story made for compelling television. What do you think the chances were for me to wrestle the remote control away to check the hockey scores when the tiger cub drama was unfolding?

So, we've talked about the economy, and we've talked about how the media gets your attention. Let's talk about the stock market.

Right now we are in a "bear market." That's the term used when the stock market comes down by at least twenty percent. Renowned industry veteran Nick Murrays says that there are really just four truths that you need to know about bear markets.

First, bear markets are a normal and natural part of a never-ending cycle. As long as the stock market follows the economy, and in the long-term that is the only thing that it can do, and as long as human nature doesn't change, which it won't, we will have bear markets.

The consequence of these things is that the stock market cycles around a constantly rising trend line. We have these cycles because people alternatively get too euphoric when times are good and too terrified when times aren't as good. Basically what happens is that when times are good, people get overly optimistic. When times aren't so good people get overly-pessimistic. The trend line is the average of these excesses. In other words, bear markets are perfectly ordinary events, just as bull markets are.

The second truth to know is that, in addition to being ordinary, bear markets are essential to the long term outperformance of the stock market. It's because of bear markets that investors demand a risk premium on their investment. If stocks were not volatile, then their prices, and thus their returns, would be bid down to a GIC-type performance range. The reason that the long-term returns after inflation for stocks are three times that of bonds is because the market demands it to compensate for the volatility.

The third truth to know is that bear markets are as common as dirt. We have had thirteen of them since the end of the Second World War. We see a bear market roughly every five years. Nobody can tell you in advance when they will start, or when they will finish, but they average out to be about a 30 percent decline, and usually last about 15 or 16 months. Right now some stock markets are down about 40 percent, and we are one year into this bear market. Chances are we are now in the final phase.

This also means that we will have another bear market in another 5 years or so. Get used to the idea. With a bear market every five years you might see five or six of them during your retirement. Again, they are as common as dirt.

Here's the fourth truth. Bear markets are always the temporary interruption of a permanent uptrend. Always.

Right now there are people that think the world is going to stop spinning on its axis, and start turning backwards, causing the sun to rise in the west and set in the east. That's not going to happen. There are always people that think that the world is coming to an end each and every time that we see a bear market.

When I started putting this essay together the Standard and Poors Index was at about 1000. The night before the first bear market following World War II, in May 1946, the S&P closed at 19.3.

Think about that. In each of these bear markets a bunch of people thought that the world had stopped spinning. This is not an exaggeration. The last bear market we had was the implosion of the tech bubble in 2001/2002. Many of you will remember that. Remember how spooky it was? Every one of these bear markets has something that spooks people. Spooky enough that people thought that this time it was different.

And yet, despite the fear and uncertainty that accompanied these bear markets, despite the fact that the world was allegedly going to stop spinning 13 times since World War II, the market is up from about 20 to 1000, not including dividends. Bear markets are always the temporary interruption of a permanent uptrend.

Here's something else that you need to know. In the past 12 bear markets, the lows that were reached were never seen again. Chances are, when this thing bottoms out, you will never see these prices again.

You know what a bear market really is? It's an extended period of time during which the people who think that this time it's different sell all their common stocks at prices that will never be seen again to people who understand that this time it's never different.

From October 2008

■ ■ ■ ■ ■ ■

Underestimating the Severity of Your Own Situation

I THINK THAT IT IS HUMAN NATURE to underestimate the severity of your own situation.

In my own life I started putting on some weight in my thirties. It was no big deal, I thought. And I did nothing about it. I still ate everything that I wanted, and I wanted a lot.

But my metabolism was naturally slowing down, and I wasn't as active anymore. In my forties I was blessed with a couple of little babies. With a desk job, and even less time for exercise, my weight went up even more.

Still, I didn't think too much about my weight. Until I had a routine health exam, and there were some anomalous results.

It took a while for it to sink in. At first I made some modest adjustments in my lifestyle. But when token efforts did nothing to change the situation I finally understood the severity of my own situation. I couldn't continue to live a sedentary lifestyle and neglect my health, without eventually having consequences.

For the first 40 years of my life I was ignorant about calories. I mean, I kind of knew what they were, but I had no idea how many I was supposed to consume to live a healthy lifestyle. I simply ate when I was hungry, and often when I wasn't, and I ate stuff that tasted good, regardless of how bad it was for me.

Now I pay closer attention to my diet. I'm far from perfect, but I'm a lot better than I was. And I'm the lightest that I've been since my twenties.

The thing about it is, it took me a decade to understand the path I was on. For years I knew that I was packing a few extra pounds around, but I rationalized it to myself. Packing around those extra pounds wasn't comfortable, but I became comfortable with it. It's not that bad, I thought, when really it kind of was.

I just feel so much better without the extra girth. I had to buy some new clothes because the old ones were falling off me. I can do things at Tae Kwan Do that I used to struggle with. I feel great.

I really should have dropped the weight years ago, but I didn't because I underestimated the severity of the situation. When I eventually realized that I was compromising my health I finally got serious about my lifestyle. I want to see my future grandkids grow up, and without taking better care of myself that might not have happened.

People underestimate the severity of their own situation all the time. People are overweight, but don't think it's that bad. People know the health risks, but continue to smoke. People drink, but they don't think they drink that much. People don't get pre-nuptial agreements because they think that their blissful situation is permanent. And people are especially good at underestimating the severity of their own situation when it comes to their finances.

People aren't putting away any money for retirement, but think that they still have time. Well, if you aren't putting money away now, what are you going to live off of later? And if you aren't putting away money now, are you going to put away enough later to catch up for the lost years? Do you know how much retirement income you are on track for? Do you know if that is going to be enough?

People have boatloads of debt, but think that their situation is under control. Maybe you can find a way to squeeze by living paycheque to paycheque now, but can you deal with the situation if it changes? What if your income dips? Can you afford your debt once interest rates inevitably rise? Could your finances deal with an emergency, like a health scare? Do you even know what you spend money on each month?

People have a small insurance policy and think that they are adequately covered. Do you know what your widow and orphaned children would really need if you were out of the picture? What would happen to the family if your income wasn't there anymore?

Or maybe there is something else that is important to you; educating your kids, caring for aged parents, building a retirement home, taking care of a disabled child, leaving a legacy, or even simply not having to worry about money anymore. The point is, understand your options, and get to work. Very few things in life fall into place through blind luck.

For me the wakeup call was when my medical tests started to come back with unusual results. Don't wait for your own wake-up call. Sometimes you don't get one.

Don't be like the young and foolish Brad, and underestimate the severity of your own situation. Be like the enlightened Brad. Understand your situation and act accordingly.

What's important to you, and what are you going to do about it?

From January 2012

The Five-Year-Old High School Graduate

I REMEMBER HER as this adorable little five-year old girl. That is, until I just saw her high school grad picture.

I know the family, but we aren't close. Just the occasional "hi" when we bump into each other at the mall, that sort of thing. And since I haven't seen this girl for years I still think of her as being five years old, even though she hasn't been five for more than a decade.

I don't know where the time goes, but I sure know that it does.

One of the things that sometimes happens when it comes to getting stuff done is the tendency to wait "until the right time". And when it comes right down to it, if you are really and truly determined to procrastinate, it's actually quite easy to put things off "until the right time".

As an example, when it comes to financial matters one of the things that is often on the to-do list, but somehow never seems to get addressed, is to get a will. It's amazing how many times I ask people if they have a will, and the answer is "Ya, I've been meaning to do that for a while now."

Given that death is something that we all have a 100% chance of experiencing, it's interesting that many people want to ensure that their affairs are in order, but "just don't have the time right now". So if you don't have the time to do it now, when will you have the time?

Don't get me wrong, I procrastinate too. I do it all the time, as a matter of fact. I moved into a new house three years ago, and I finally got around to hanging pictures last month. And it wasn't even me who hung the pics. I had my Dad do it for me when he was up visiting.

But there is a significant difference in importance in how long it takes to get around to hanging a picture and how long it takes to get around to taking care of your finances.

The point of this essay is that time waits for nobody. And when it comes to money matters, often you can't afford to wait. One day you wake up and 5-year olds are graduating from high school.

To quote the great philosopher Theodor Geisel (aka Dr. Seuss), in his timeless classic "*Oh, the Places You'll Go!*" The 'Waiting Place' is a most useless place, where everyone is…

> "Waiting for the fish to bite
> or waiting for the wind to fly a kite
> or waiting around for Friday night
> or waiting, perhaps, for their Uncle Jake
> or a pot to boil, or a Better Break
> or a string of pearls, or a pair of pants
> or a wig with curls, or Another Chance.
> Everyone is just waiting."

And, of course, when a person is in the waiting place nothing is happening. It's not until our hero escapes all that waiting and staying that he finds the bright places where Boom Bands are playing.

What about you? Are you waiting around for Friday night, or your Uncle Jake, or a pot to boil, or a better break, and all the while it really is time to get moving?

Sure, once in a while it might make sense to wait until the planets are in perfect alignment before undertaking a course of action, but generally speaking you really can't wait for the perfect time to bump up your mortgage payment, or to start putting money away for your grandkid's education, or to get your will updated, or whatever it is that is important to you.

You can't wait for the "perfect time." The perfect time may never arrive. And if it does arrive, you might find that by that time the window of opportunity has closed.

Rather than waiting for the perfect time, what you can do is make incremental changes. Maybe it's not the perfect time to try to double your mortgage payment, but perhaps you can bump it up by $50 bucks a month. Maybe it's not the perfect time to invest for your future, but perhaps you can find $100 per month to put away.

Just get started on something. You'll be amazed at the cumulative impact of incremental changes over a person's lifetime. But get going now, before you wake up one day and realize your five year old baby just graduated from high school.

From July 2011

■ ■ ■ ■ ■ ■

This Is Not Diversification

I AM PRETTY COMFORTABLE in assuming that most readers have heard the expression, "Don't put all your eggs in one basket." But on the off chance that the phrase is unfamiliar, it simply means that if a person is to diversify their investments (so that they have a number of things on the go rather than having all their wealth concentrated), then they should be able to reduce the chances of a catastrophic event affecting the entirety of their wealth.

The wisdom of diversification is commonly accepted, and proper diversification really is a wonderful thing. But the problem is that some people take the expression "Don't put all your eggs in one basket" to heart, without truly understanding what meaningful diversification really is. If that happens then the best result that you could hope for would be benign confusion, but it is not uncommon for the investor to make perilous errors in a well-meaning, but flawed, attempt at placing their eggs in multiple baskets.

When it comes to diversification mistakes, on the less serious end of the scale we have simply taken things to excess. Statistically you can have meaningful diversification with as little as twenty or so individual stocks. Once your portfolio is adequately diversified there is little marginal benefit to add more and more positions to your portfolio. In fact, if you continue to add more and more holdings to your portfolio then once you reach a certain point, rather than reducing risk, you are far more likely to simply be diluting the quality of your holdings. This is no longer diversification, its di-worse-ification.

Di-worse-ification is when you stop diversifying and start duplicating more of what you already own. If you find yourself spreading $50,000 over 14 mutual funds you have likely long since passed the point of adequate diversification, and now all you are doing is adding complexity. But also inevitably you end up with your second or third best ideas. Why not focus on the investments that hold the most promise?

Di-worse-ification isn't great, but I don't see it as particularly dangerous. It's merely sloppy, inefficient and lacking in purpose.

Potentially even more problematic is diversifying by advisor. Some people will choose to work with more than one advisor. Occasionally there is good reason for this. If you have sophisticated needs there is nothing wrong with working with a tax planning specialist and an investment specialist and an insurance specialist, particularly when everyone knows their role and works co-operatively as a team.

Far more common though is to have a bunch of people all trying to do the same thing, and the results can be chaotic. Recently I had a client's bank call me about trying to reverse a Tax Free Savings Account contribution from 2010 because, on the advice of the banker, the client had made subsequent future Tax Free Savings Account contributions and was now in an overcontribution situation and facing penalties from CRA.

I don't know why the client ended up with multiple TFSAs, but this type of diversifying by advisor isn't really putting eggs in different baskets. It's more like randomly throwing eggs at baskets and hoping that they land safely.

I don't know where things went sideways here. Did the banker not ask the client about their TFSA contribution room? Did the client not understand that they already had a TFSA? In the end, it doesn't really matter what the mistake was, the point is that having multiple people advise you on the same thing can result in unexpected and unpleasant consequences.

Personally I think the only sensible approach is to find the advisor that is the best fit for you and to engage them with a partnership mentality. But failing that, at least let all your advisors know what you expect of them. It's not mandatory that you work with only one advisor, but you pretty much need someone to quarterback your financial plan lest you risk breaking the very eggs that you were trying to protect.

From June 2013

Real Advice Doesn't Come from a Magazine

I WAS LOOKING THROUGH an old magazine from 2010 the other day and I came across an article that prescribed seven specific stocks to buy. What a load of malarkey.

I'm not saying these stock picks were bad investments. I actually have no idea what their past performance has been.

What I'm saying is that you can't get true advice from a magazine. Not personalized advice that is specific to your situation anyway. There is a very simple reason for that. The author doesn't know you, and he isn't writing with you specifically in mind.

Here's what I mean. Let's say that you are feeling a little run down lately, so you start looking through some medical journals for some answers. You have a fever, you are feeling weak. Your body hurts, and you are just so darn tired. So what's wrong?

Well, depending on what article you are reading you might convince yourself that you are suffering from anything from the flu to a snake bite. Clearly the appropriate medical treatment will differ significantly depending on the correct diagnosis, but you can't get diagnosis from a magazine.

Were those seven stock picks appropriate? Only if the reader had the appropriate objectives, risk tolerance, account size, and financial knowledge. In other words, the picks might be fine for some readers, but they might be quite inappropriate for others, and the article doesn't distinguish between the two groups.

Real advice will be specific to your own situation. For example, recently I had the pleasure of meeting a young lady in her twenties. I have worked with her grandparents for some time, and they suggested that she come in to see me.

She's highly educated, with an excellent, well-paying career. She has no debt, and she has a little extra money to put away towards something each month. She is in a high tax bracket, and is concerned that her retirement savings through her employer will be inadequate. So what should she do with her money?

Well, there are a ton of articles out there that would instruct this person to invest for growth because of her age and objectives, and make the investment inside her retirement savings plan for the tax savings. I have written many of these types of articles myself. Getting an early start is just such a huge mathematical advantage. Its compound growth in a tax friendly environment, baby. The more time you have, the more money you end up with.

The only problem with this boilerplate type advice is that the person needs to be in the exact situation that the author is writing about for the advice to be appropriate.

An article that proclaims that people in their 20's and in a high tax bracket should simply invest for growth using the retirement savings plan would be more useful if it included the disclaimer that it is only applicable as long as there aren't any exceptions that trump the original advice. Exceptions could be: You are drowning in debt that you need to deal with first. You don't have the necessary retirement savings plan contribution room to execute the strategy. Your risk tolerance approaches paranoia and you can't cope with daily, fractional volatility. Your health is compromised. Your job is not stable. Etcetera.

But a magazine article can't really include all the potential exceptions. It's just not feasible. And in this particular case, there is an exception in play. You see, on further examination, this lady also wants to buy her first house.

So we are going to use the retirement savings plan, alright. But we aren't investing for growth. We are investing for liquidity, with the intention of removing the funds from her retirement savings plan tax-free under the Home Buyer's Plan.

Magazines are great for discussing ideas. They can be a source of some good information. But for specific advice, talk to a professional.

From August 2013

■ ■ ■ ■ ■ ■

Are You an Investor or a Speculator?

MY GIRLFRIEND AND I just got back from a wonderful vacation in the Dominican Republic. We stayed at a beach-front resort, the weather was great, and I even went scuba diving for the first time.

Ironically, the day before I left, the markets went into a dizzying tailspin. In fact, the front page headline in the National Post was "LOST TRILLION ECLIPSES BLACK MONDAY – Market carnage costs U.S. shareholders almost $1-trillion, Canadians $50-billion."

One might think that these dramatic headlines detracted from my tropical vacation. Actually, I barely thought about it at all. How can this be? With the Toronto Stock Exchange falling 5.5% in a single day, why was I not monitoring CNBC, checking the internet for news, trying to analyze every nuance of these frantic events.

I'll tell you why. BECAUSE THIS HAPPENS ALL THE TIME! As much as my colleagues in the media like to write dramatic headlines, the simple truth of the matter is that 5 per cent drops in the stock market happen every one or two years. They are not new, and they are not cause for concern for the true long-term investor.

By the way, there is no such thing as a short-term investor. If you are investing in the stock market with a time horizon shorter than five years, you are a speculator, not an investor. Speculators get creamed by 5 per cent market declines. True investors love market declines.

No lie! If you are a true investor you relish the opportunity to pick up shares in world class companies at bargain prices. Every once in a while the stock market has a big sale. Speculators call these events crashes, corrections, or adjustments. Investors call them opportunities.

Let's say you wanted to buy a pair of jeans. The jeans usually sell for $50, but today they are on sale for $30. What are you going to do? Get out the chequebook, of course. You have the opportunity to pick up a quality product at a super price, and that makes sense.

Let's say you wanted to buy a piece of a great business. Shares in the business usually sell for $50, but today you have the opportunity to buy a piece of this great business for $30. A speculator dwells on the "correction" from $50 to $30. An investor gets out the chequebook.

Tell me what makes more sense – accumulating shares in a great business at wonderful prices like a long-term investor, or lingering over stale and near-sighted views on stock market volatility like a speculator.

By the way, the last thing I did before I caught the plane to the Dominican Republic was put more money in my favourite equity mutual fund. Because I am a long-term investor, and April 15, 2000 was a great opportunity.

From May 2000

Now Is the Time to Repair Your Roof

HERE'S A SIMPLE TRUTH that every investor needs to know: any investment that has the potential for above-average returns has the potential to disappoint you.

The majority of investors have only been investing for the last five or six years. For the most part, they have only experienced good times. This will not go on indefinitely.

Sure, we have had some crazy events recently – the Asian Flu in 1998, Russian and Brazilian currency woes in 1999, fears of interest rate hikes in the USA. But most investors do not have firsthand experience with a prolonged bear market. I am talking about a long, painful experience – perhaps the markets declining by 30 to 50 percent over 12 to 18 months.

First, the good news. There are no indications that we are about to enter a recession. In fact, it's hard to imagine economic conditions being much better.

Second, the bad news. Although stock markets present outstanding investment opportunities over the long term, the stock markets do not have a high degree of reliability from month to month. What this means is that even though conditions seem to be great, there can be no promise that some unforeseen event does not come along to upset the apple cart.

I believe we are going to continue to see outstanding investment returns. I also believe that the investments that have been providing the outstanding returns of today are probably not going to be the same investments that provide the outstanding investment returns of tomorrow.

For anyone who has exposure to the real high-octane stuff, imagine the next investment statement you receive is worth half as much as your last statement. If you have a hard time with this, it is time to examine your portfolio.

Know your investment; know what you own and why you own it. Know the risks involved, and know what to do when we see the inevitable next round of market volatility.

Ever heard the expression that the time to repair your roof is when the sun is shining? Well, the sun is shining now. And something I know for sure is that it's better to look at your portfolio before the next big market decline rather than surveying the damage after the fact.

From March 2000

Quit Crying and Get Off the Sideline

I RECALL AN ESSAY that I wrote more than a year ago when the magnitude of the stock market malaise first became apparent. I said that while the length and depth of this bear market is unknowable, there would come a time when the investors smart enough to take advantage of the buying opportunities that would inevitably be presented would be well-rewarded.

I think that time is now. Serious money is made in bear markets. It just takes some time for this to be realized.

Before I tell you why I think the current market environment is one of the rare opportunities that come around every couple of market cycles, let me begin with a word of caution. Not every asset is a bargain.

In April Nortel was trading at $6.00. At that time I wrote that I was not convinced that business was one that I wanted to own. Now Nortel is under $1.50, and I still have the same opinion. I'm told that they have cash for about 6 months of operations, and it's getting harder for them to raise funds. Maybe Nortel will turn around, maybe it will go bankrupt. Personally, I don't see Nortel as an opportunity.

But there certainly are opportunities that do abound. Although it doesn't feel that way, it's true.

As John Templeton says, the four most dangerous words are "this time it's different." This bear market is not different from previous ones, and all bear markets come to an end eventually.

Here is why I think it's time to consider putting some money to work now. Not after the TSX breaks 7000. Now.

First, you don't get that many chances. Recently the Dow gained 8 percent in a single week. Right out of the blue, just like most stock market rallies. Anybody who was not invested missed out.

Second, the best returns come at the start of bull markets, when many investors are still bearish. In the 15 bear markets since 1950 the S&P 500 earned between 15 percent and 40 percent in the 12 months after the bear ended.

Third, stocks outperform everything else over the long term. Let's say that two people had 100,000 to invest at the end of the terrible bear market of 1973-1974. One person puts his money in term deposits. At the end of 2001 he has $832,000. The second person puts half of her money in term deposits and half in the S&P 500. She finishes with $3.1 million.

Fourth, painful bear markets don't last indefinitely. If you had bought right before the terrible bear market of 1972 you would have seen your investment down by 42.6 percent at the worst point, but you would have recovered your money by 1976.

What should a long-term investor do? Diversify, dollar-cost average, and stay the course.

What should a serious long-term investor comfortable with variability do? Get off the couch and put some money to work while this golden opportunity lasts.

From August 2002

Why I Hope the Stock Market Goes Down

ON THE DAY THAT I AM WRITING this article the Toronto Stock Exchange 300 index went down by about two percent. The TSE 300 is down about ten percent from its all time high set earlier this year.

I think this is just great.

The only thing that would be better is if it went down even more.

I am not being sarcastic, and I do not exhibit sadomasochistic tendencies. Well, okay maybe a bit of sadomasochism, as I am a Vancouver Canucks fan, and that has been a fairly painful experience over the last several years.

But back to the stock market. Why do I want the stock market to go down?

The answer is simple. It's because I am not done buying.

Here's something that has been overlooked far too often in the last year or so. The stock market is not a lottery ticket. It's not a casino. It's not bingo hall. The stock market is not any sort of get rich quick scheme, even though the guy your brother works with hit it big by buying Ballard Power at $56.

Yes, it is true there is anecdotal evidence that the stock market can make a person an overnight millionaire. Now here is the reason that you better not confuse speculating with investing. It's because speculating means just that, and sometimes the results you hope for are not necessarily the results you get. Just ask anyone who bought Nortel at $120.

By the way, the real driver of stock price is corporate profitability. If you own a company that is making money, sooner or later that will be reflected in the share price. If you own a company that is losing money, that too will be reflected in the stock price sooner or later.

So if the stock market is not a foolproof way to get rich overnight, what is it? Well, it's just as the name says. It is a market for stocks – a place where you can buy an ownership interest in different businesses.

What a wonderful idea! The stock market is a place where we can buy a little piece of some fabulous businesses. And as those businesses grow and prosper, we, as the rightful owners of those businesses, get to participate in their profitability.

So let's say you want to buy a business, or anything else for that matter. Do you want to pay a high price, or a low price for what you are buying? A low price, of course.

If you are having a barbecue and you go to the store to buy some steak, do you want to pay a high price for the steak? Of course not. If you are buying a vehicle do you tell the salesman that you insist on paying full price for the vehicle? Of course not. If you want to buy a company do you want to pay an inflated price for the shares? Of course not. So stock market pullbacks can mean buying opportunities.

Sometimes people say "Yes, but what if it doesn't come back? What if the stock stays low forever?" These people are thinking like speculators, not like investors.

If you have a chance to acquire a solid company, in good shape now and with good prospects for the future, and on top of all this, to acquire it a bargain price, well that sound you hear is the sound of opportunity knocking.

Bear in mind that I am talking about buying fabulous companies at cheap prices. I am not talking about buying companies in distress just because the shares are cheap. If a company is about to enter into receivership I don't care how cheap the shares get, I don't want any.

Sometimes an opportunity comes up when you can buy shares in fabulous companies that generate significant profit and you can buy them at bargain prices. A great example is Black Monday – on October 19, 1987, the stock markets fell by more than twenty percent.

Was the world really any different on October 20, 1987, than it was on October 18, 1987? No, not really. Except now you could pick up shares in your favourite companies twenty-percent cheaper than you could get them for just a few days previously. Speculators called this a market crash; investors called it a twenty-percent off sale.

Was October 20, 1987 a buying opportunity? Absolutely, without doubt, no question about it, somebody tell the band the parade is about to begin, and we ain't waiting for stragglers.

Hey, I have some great news for anyone who is looking to build their long-term wealth! The stock market is down! Now you have the opportunity to acquire some wonderful businesses at bargain prices!

The only thing that would make me happier is if the stock market would go down even more. Then I could buy some wonderful businesses even cheaper yet!

From September 2000

The Secret to Financial Success

THERE IS ONE THING that is of primary importance on the road to financial success. It's not your income, or your Retirement Savings Plans, or home ownership, or negotiating a better interest rate from your bank. The most important thing that determines whether a person will be financially successful is controlling your cash flow.

What do I mean by controlling your cash flow? Very simple: spend less than you earn, and put a little bit away for the future. Like many good ideas though, the fact that controlling your cash flow is simple doesn't mean that it is easy to do.

There is a lot of temptation out there, and it's all too easy to spend a little more than a person should. As a matter of fact, it's jolly good fun to go into debt – that big screen TV that you don't pay for until next spring, that vacation that gets charged to your credit card, that new vehicle with those low monthly payments. Getting into debt is fun!

Getting out of debt, on the other hand, is a different story. There's no joy involved in struggling to get out of debt. And getting out of debt can take years.

It can be so very tempting to splurge, to treat yourself, to rationalize that you really do need something bright and shiny. Bright and shiny things are fun. But too many splurges can put a pretty serious kink in your finances, not just now, as you struggle to pay for these bright and shiny things, but later on as well.

Too much debt makes it that much harder to reach your financial objectives. Having monthly loan obligations means that the money needed to service those loans can't be used for something else, something that increases your net worth. Meanwhile, think of the interest payments on your loans as your money disappearing is a puff of smoke.

People sometimes call me, looking for help after they realize that things have gotten out of control. And these people have one thing in common. It's not necessarily age, or occupation, or lifestyle choices that these people have in common. No, the trait that they all share is that they are miserable.

Being up to your eyes in debt, to use the colloquialism, sucks. Obviously it keeps you from accomplishing the things that you want to do, but it also is extremely stressful – both for yourself, and for those around you. The misery of the downtrodden debtor.

Here's the thing that the "buy now, pay later", instant gratification mentality sweeps under the carpet: There is a price to pay for our spending decisions, and the price can be steep. People who choose to live beyond their means while they are working are likely going to pay a hefty price during their golden years for their spendthrift ways.

Here's the scenario: During a person's working life they spent money like a campaigning politician. They lived in a house that they couldn't afford, leased new vehicles every couple or three years, bought expensive things that sat unused in the closet gathering dust. They couldn't go through money faster if they set it on fire. The family budget is on life-support. Every penny of income, plus a little borrowed money to boot, gets staked in the perennial game of "Why shouldn't I get it now?"

Okay, now it's the end of the working years. It's time to put our feet up on the porch and enjoy the view. The only problem is that nothing has been saved and there is not enough cash flow to sustain the lifestyle. And now we are looking at pretty severe lifestyle adjustments.

By foregoing smart financial planning during the working years, when a person has both time and resources on their side, many people are going to be in for a rude awakening when they realize that they are staring at retirement with depleted savings. What was supposed to be a time of leisure suddenly looks pretty bleak, with few decades of retirement ahead and little to draw on.

If these people do not change their spending habits now retirement is going to seem more like purgatory than a time for relaxation and leisure. This is not a melodramatic statement. The average Canadian baby boomer carries 5 to 10 credit cards, and yet 42 percent of Canadians have no savings.

This would be less of a problem if people were both willing and able to work their entire lifetime. However, 66 percent of Canadians want to retire before age 65.

To be brutally frank, a very large number of Canadians need a reality check. We have all these people who want to retire, but they have no idea how this is going to happen.

Of these people that you would think would be, at a bare minimum, giving some amount of thought towards retirement, never mind actively preparing for it, 79 percent of people do not have a retirement plan, and 59 percent say that they are behind in saving for retirement.

I don't know how much more clearly I can state this. If you aren't preparing for retirement, then don't expect much of one. Sure you can retire without any savings of your own, but it won't be an early retirement, or a luxurious one.

In our area we have quite a few people who make (and spend) a lot of money. Here's the thing though; being "rich" is not a retirement plan. In fact, wealthier people have been found to be at even greater risk of facing an unpleasant and startling decline in their income at retirement. Simply put, very few high-income earners save enough to maintain their standard of living through retirement.

Many people who would generally be considered well off rely on their enviable salaries to pay for their daily bread with Grey Poupon. So what do these people do when those enviable salaries are no longer there?

One of the biggest problems is complacency. Even people who have high incomes are unaware of the need for retirement planning. That's a mistake. You don't have to make it. Prepare for retirement now.

A retirement plan looks at how much you can reasonably spend, how you should invest so that you don't outlive your savings, and how much you can reasonably leave behind for your family or favourite charity.

Live within your means, and squirrel a little away for the future. That's the key to financial success.

From March 2007

PART SIX

Please Just Tell Me Things Are Going to Be OK

The number one fear for people heading
into retirement is running out of money.

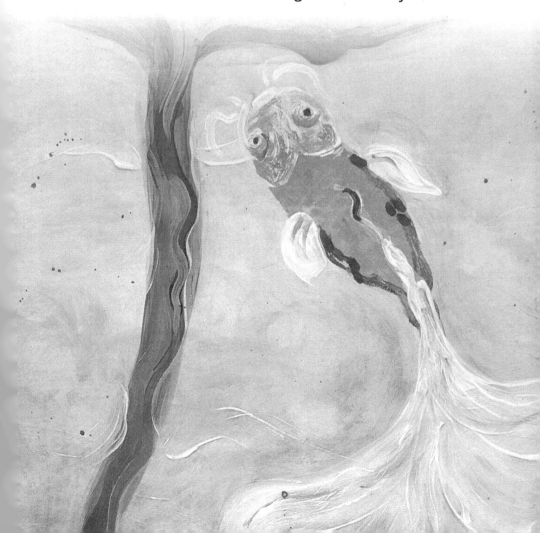

·······

What I Have Learned in 225 Weekly Essays

I LIKE WRITING THESE ESSAYS. It means that each week I have to research an idea, and put some thoughts together in a somewhat coherent fashion.

As I look back on the ghosts of essays past, I see various things. Some predictions that turned out well, and some that didn't. Given the luxury of hindsight and journalistic license I can pick out some important messages, which were occasionally heeded by readers, but also sometimes ignored. Some of these stories are anecdotal, and some are backed up by scientific study. Here are some lessons from the last 225 essays.

Y2K caused a tremendous amount of fear, but no major problems. Real disasters don't give you advance warning. If you have advance warning you can take steps to avert a disaster. We were prepared for Y2K. We were not prepared for September 11, accounting scandals, SARS, or mad cows.

Many people don't bother with insurance until after something bad happens.

All the charts and statistics and historical evidence in the world do not mean a thing if a person has no faith in capitalism. Many investors believed themselves to be long-term investors, but they really meant that they could tolerate modest volatility as long as the inevitable market downturn is no worse than a 20 percent decline and shorter than 6 months in duration.

New Year's Resolutions are buried by March, only to be resurrected in December.

People can parrot "buy low, sell high" from now until the next ice age, but they will still buy tech stocks in 1999, and they will sell quality investments in 2003. When a balanced fund has a one-year rate of return of eighty percent (it really did happen) people want to buy it. When a solid investment has a two-year negative return people want to get out at any cost.

"This time it's different" is the most dangerous expression in the world when it comes to investing.

The pain that comes from watching your investment account balance shrink hurts far worse than the pleasure derived from making money when times are good.

It is easy to recognize market peaks, but far harder to acknowledge market bottoms.

Only engineers or teachers read prospectuses. Most everyone else considers them junk mail, even if they do describe all the stuff you should really know at least a little bit about before you invest.

Many people who buy stock on their own volition really have no clue about the company they are buying a piece of. The opinion of the guy with the loudest voice in the coffee room carries more weight than fundamental research. Not only that, these same people absolutely have to buy stock in the next five minutes because they believe the share price will double any second, and they don't want to miss out. This supposed ticket to riches that they absolutely must have is very, very rarely a solid blue-chip company, but rather some speculative penny stock that ends up disappointing them 19 times out of 20.

Many people think they can accurately perform feats of market timing. Despite that, of the billions of people that have walked on this earth since industrial revolution, not one of which has yet to demonstrate that they can consistently time the markets, people still think that they have some gift of Midas that will lead them to vast riches.

Many readers will not recognize their own behavior as they read this essay. In the immortal words of Charlie Munger, "I have nothing to add."

From September 2003

■ ■ ■ ■ ■ ■

How to Not Screw Up Your Life

Just now I was consulting with my associate Meagan on a situation where some people have found themselves in a jam, and she says, "You know, we need to petition the B.C. government to educate people starting in Grade 7 about how to not screw up your life."

"Ah ha, that's the next essay," I said.

There's that old expression "Money isn't everything." That is 100 percent correct. Money isn't everything. But more often than not, the people who find themselves saying that "money isn't everything" don't have any.

That can be perfectly okay. It's fine to have priorities that go beyond material wealth. It's commendable even.

Where trouble starts – and it starts fast – is when people say money isn't everything, but their spending behavior is more consistent with money being the only thing.

If you want to make a decision to focus on other things – maybe work less so that you can spend more time with the kids – that's great. Not only do I think that's a phenomenal idea, I am envious. I want to spend more time with my family too.

But – and this is a big but – if you decide to work less, then your spending behavior has to reflect your reduced income. I run into lots of people who make $8000 per month, but spend ten.

For a lot of people $8000 a month is a lot of money. Having a healthy income will often give a person a false sense of security. Sure making a lot of money means that you get to spend more money, but it doesn't matter how much you make, you still can't continually spend beyond your income and expect things to work themselves out.

So the first rule for not screwing up your life is to live within your means. And if your means change – as they have done recently for a lot of people given the economic slowdown – then it is likely that you will have to make adjustments to your spending behavior.

Another rule is to know your priorities. New trucks are shiny, but they don't stay new for long. Put first things first. A $1200 per month truck payment is going to mean $1200 that can't be spent on something else – perhaps something more important in the long run.

When it comes to priorities, there isn't one right answer. The point is that you want to work towards what's important to you, whatever that happens to be. If the most important thing in the world to you is having a brand new truck, well, you are in luck. There are some good deals out there.

On the other hand, if you can get by without spending $65,000 on something that starts depreciating as soon as you drive it off the lot, then that's something to give some thought to before you commit to five years worth of hefty truck payments.

Pay yourself first. Each month people want your money. The taxman wants some. Your bank wants some. Utility companies want some. Your cell phone provider and cable company want some. Restaurants and entertainment providers want some. Everybody wants your money.

And while some or all of these people will get part of your money each month, none of them is more important than you are. Each month take part of your income – 10 percent is a starting spot – and put it away for the future.

Living on the remaining 90 percent of your income is not likely to be a noticeable difference in your standard of living today. If you fail to prepare for the future, however, you most certainly will notice a difference in your standard of living down the road.

Be strategic, not impulsive, with your money decisions. Being impulsive with big ticket purchases can lead to poor decisions. We've all done it. I'm the first to admit it. I've got a $700 wood chipper in my shed that I've still only used a couple of times.

Heck, I even bought a house on impulse once. Sometimes a person needs to step back and ask themselves if what they think they really, really want is actually something that they need.

Know the difference between good debt and bad debt. Good debt is something that you take on in order to help get something important done.

The best debt would be for an asset that appreciates over time, carries a low interest rate, and if its tax deductible that's even better.

Bad debt is debt for lifestyle expenditures or on a depreciating asset, carries a high rate of interest, and isn't tax deductible. Most consumer loans are examples of bad debt. If you have bad debt, work hard to pay it off, or see if you can convert it to good debt.

Pay less tax. There are many legitimate ways to pay less tax. Take advantage of them. Appeal your property tax assessment. Accumulate assets in tax-assisted vehicles. Save your medical and charitable donation receipts. Have your taxes prepared by a qualified person so that you don't miss any opportunities.

Prepare for your kids future education. It's going to be expensive, and they are going to need it. Down the road people won't just walk into careers. There will always be jobs, but careers are what provide more satisfaction and better compensation, and careers require training.

Protect your income. Fundamental to almost everything you want to do in life is that you have cash coming in. If your cash flow stops, everything else might too. Make sure that you have good income protection plans in place that mitigate the financial consequences of disability, critical illness, and premature death, and do what you can to protect yourself from unemployment or under-employment.

So far we've talked about just money issues. After all, this is an essay about money. But if I'm writing a primer on how to not screw up your life I'd better mention your health too. Take care of yourself. It's the only body that you'll ever have. Abuse it now and you'll notice it later.

Finally, keep things in balance. Don't go overboard in one area of your life to the extent that other important things are neglected. You can't live completely for today and ignore the future, but life is pretty dull if you sacrifice everything today for a day that might never come.

If people follow these rules I think they will do a pretty good job of not screwing up their life. Its true money isn't everything, but you still want to have some cash in the bank when you say that.

From July 2009

■ ■ ■ ■ ■ ■

The Stock Market Roller Coaster

I SAW A TV AD for a brand new roller coaster at some theme park today, which was an interesting coincidence. Given the recent volatility in investment markets I have been thinking about roller coasters lately.

A roller coaster ride can be thrilling. Even a little scary. There is usually a fair bit of screaming involved, either from the thrill or the fear.

We see the same type of reactions from investment roller coasters. It can be thrilling. It can be scary. In either case, lots of screaming is not unusual.

Right now some people are thinking the stock market is going to go off the rails, and the best thing to do is to try to jump out to safety. Just like on a real roller coaster ride, though, trying to jump off halfway through the ride is a good way to get hurt.

For the stock market – roller coaster analogy to work we have to assume some things. One of the primary assumptions is that the roller coaster is the right ride for you in the first place.

If you really should never have gotten on the roller coaster to start with, then this essay isn't geared for you. There are probably some people out there who ended up in the roller coaster line when they should have queued for the merry-go-round, but that's a different conversation.

So why would a person choose the thrills and chills of the roller coaster over the predictability of the merry-go-round? Simple. The roller coaster goes faster.

In the investment world, equities are the roller coaster and Guaranteed Investment Certificates are the merry-go-round. Equities give you better performance (in other words, more speed in your portfolio) over the long term, but they have ups and downs along the way. GICs are slower, but they move along in a predictable way.

Sometimes the decision to get in line for the roller coaster is less of a choice than a necessity. More speed (in other words, better long-term returns) is needed to achieve the objective. A common example is retirement income planning. Often the merry-go-round, although predictable, just simply isn't moving fast enough to allow you to accumulate enough money to retire on time and with the lifestyle you desire.

The good news for people who need the speed of the roller coaster to achieve a goal (such as sustainable income in retirement), but who would be more comfortable on something like a merry-go-round, there are some options. We can slow the roller coaster down. We can give you a helmet and extra seat belts.

Roller coaster rides can be scary, but they can also be thrilling. The investors who are going to be thrilled with these current lower prices for investments are the ones who are taking advantage of them. Buying good quality investments at reduced prices is exciting. That's what Warren Buffett, the World's Greatest Investor, is doing right now. It's a strategy that's worked out reasonably well for him.

Still, there is a lot of screaming out there. And, for what it's worth, I think that there are still a few more ups and downs on the track ahead. But, assuming that the roller coaster is the ride with the speed you need, if you keep your seat you should arrive safely. Barring extenuating circumstances, the people who get hurt are the ones who try to jump off a roller coaster half way through the ride.

From July 2008

Doom and Gloom Everywhere

I WAS IN VICTORIA, BRITISH COLUMBIA, this past week, and while there it was my intention to write an essay about rising interest rates. It's a topic that has been in the queue for a couple weeks already, but I decided to table that one for now.

The reason for postponing an essay on interest rates, despite the widespread appeal of the mesmerizing subject matter, is because I started getting inquiries from several different people; the general theme being that there is doom and gloom everywhere.

Not for me there isn't.

So let's get everyone up to speed. You may recall that last week I wrote about the prospects for the USA defaulting on its national debt, the probability of which I placed at just about zero. Sure enough, after significant political brinkmanship from both sides, an eleventh hour compromise was found, and the latest fad crisis was averted.

In a nutshell, politicians of all stripes recognized that something needed to be done, but the Democrats thought that the solution was to borrow more money to get through the current economic malaise, while the Republicans thought that spending cuts should take priority. In the end, both sides got a little of what they wanted, but nobody was really too happy with what they got.

Which brings us to the next chapter in the story. Being of the opinion that the budget cuts did not go as far as necessary, credit rating agency Standard & Poor's downgraded the credit rating of the United States, from the laudable AAA to the almost-as-good AA+. They felt that the US had not really come up with a credible plan to tackle the nation's long-term debt.

This opinion is not without controversy.

The US Treasury claims that S&P's analysis is flawed, believing that Standard and Poor's initially miscalculated the growth trajectory of the nation's debt by $2 trillion, and then went ahead with its downgrade anyway.

Of interest is that Standard and Poor's is the only credit rating agency that downgraded the US credit rating. Rival agencies Moody's and Fitch both affirmed their highest rating for the USA.

Keep in mind that Standard and Poor's was the recent target of significant criticism over its role in the sub-prime banking catastrophe, assigning top ratings to what eventually turned out to be risky, and mostly worthless, investments. Critics say that, following a fiasco of that magnitude, their credibility for evaluating a nation's fiscal policy is seriously impaired.

It's not that Standard and Poor's concerns are groundless, however. The USA has borrowed a lot of money, and continues to do so. Structural problems with funding their health care and social safety net are unresolved. And their unemployment rate has crept into the 9 percent range.

The reaction to the S & P downgrade has been mixed. Some people see it as a wake-up call; or maybe a wake-up punch to the solar plexus might be a bit of a better description, shaking people out of their complacency regarding unfettered government largesse.

Other people don't agree with Standard and Poor's conclusion, though. And one of those people happens to be Warren Buffett. Buffett says that the S & P downgrade doesn't make sense. And he's a guy that should know. He owns more than $40 Billion in US Treasury Bills – the very securities that are affected by the credit downgrade. And with $40,000,000,000 on the table, you think he'd be a guy that would have an interest in the ability of the US government to service their debt, eh?

But not only is Buffett not selling T-bills, he just made a $3 billion offer to purchase another insurance company.

So if it really and truly is unadulterated doom and gloom out there, as some people are wont to believe, why is the World's Greatest Investor making acquisitions?

Look, nobody is really going to be thrilled about the news of a credit downgrade, but let's put this into perspective. After all, it's not the first time a country has seen a credit downgrade. In fact, it's even happened to our country, and in the not too distant past at that.

In 1993 Canada's credit rating was downgraded from AAA. By the way, in the 12 months that followed, the Toronto Stock Exchange returned more than 15 percent. That wasn't an isolated case either. Japan's credit rating was downgraded in 1998, and the Nikkei rose by 25 percent in the subsequent year.

Also, bear in mind that a downgrade is not a permanent sentence. Canada is now back in the AAA club after eventually getting its financial house more in order.

What we have right now is some people focusing on the negative. This isn't unusual. If you are bound and determined to be grumpy, it's not hard to find a reason to validate your preconceived notions. This past week it's been gloriously sunny in Victoria, which makes the pessimists happy since, while they can't grumble about rain, at least now they can fret about the increased risk of skin cancer.

Speaking of Victoria, my Dad mentioned something to me recently, and it's something that can be extraordinarily useful in wrapping your mind around these financial issues. If you really and truly understand this, you are going to be just fine.

My folks bought their home in Victoria in the late 1980s. This past week, my Dad says to me that property prices in Victoria have come down by about 10 percent in the last six months. For anyone keeping score at home, that's roughly the same results as seen by North American stock markets over the same length of time.

So, should my Dad sell his house?

I mean, if you look in the papers, there are some nasty stories about the state of the Victoria real estate market. Prices are dropping, and inventories are increasing. Tourism, long a staple of the Victorian economy, is on a multi-year slide and expectations for the future are dim. Some feature properties are not moving, even after being heavily discounted. The future for real estate is murky, even gloomy.

So should he sell?

Most rational people, not needing to know anything more than I have told you, would say "Don't sell." After all, real estate in Victoria is probably a pretty decent asset to own. So why would you sell a decent asset just because the price comes down?

If anything, maybe a person should be looking at buying a decent asset if the price comes down, eh? Buy low, right?

So, if you wouldn't sell your house after losing 10 percent in 6 months, why would you sell a diversified collection of world class businesses? And I really do mean world class. Let's say that you own shares in Coca Cola, the Royal Bank, Berkshire Hathaway, McDonalds, Wal-Mart and Microsoft, among others. If you owned these companies, why would you sell them if the prices got cheap? If anything, should a person not be looking to acquire more shares in world class businesses when the prices get cheap? Buy low, right?

After all, that's what Buffett is doing.

So, who are you going to listen to about all these goings on? The guy who always finds a reason to complain, even on a sunny day? Or the greatest investor that has ever lived?

Doom and gloom everywhere? I beg to differ, sir.

Opportunity everywhere. Bring it on!

From August 2011

■■■■■■

The Anti-Alarmist

ONE OF MY FRIENDS is a financial journalist. Recently he said "I am of the strong belief that 2012 will bring as much – or more volatility – as in 2011, but not a serious downturn. Hang on for a rough ride."

To which I immediately replied, "I am of the strong belief that for a true long-term investor what happens in 2012 (or any brief blip in time) is not material."

You see, I'm getting a little full of all the melodrama from the financial journalists. So I'm making it my job to counter the hype, the exaggeration, the making of routine events into something of permanent significance.

Call me the anti-alarmist. Folks, the world's economy is not going to vanish. Despite what the financial journalists told you.

Last year this same friend was concerned that the US stock market was going to fall off a cliff. And, no doubt, over the last year you probably heard a significant amount from the financial journalists about how bad it is in the US. Given that, you may very well be under the impression that 2011 was a really bad year for the US markets.

So, do you want to hazard a guess as to what kind of year the US really had?

The correct answer is the US markets were flat in 2011. Seriously, a flat year, that's it. 2008 was a horrible year. 2009 was a fantastic year. 2010 was perfectly acceptable. 2011 was a whole lot of nothing. Go ahead and check it out for yourself.

Call me the financial myth-buster. The US markets did not have a bad year in 2011, despite what the financial journalists told you.

It's not a surprise that people are confused about the current state of affairs. Not too long ago I heard a resident financial guru doing a market report on the radio. He tried to describe quantitative easing, a little bit of jargon that refers to a US monetary policy that has the objective of stimulating the US economy.

The only problem is the guy messed up his explanation. In fact, he got things completely backwards. Whether this was simply a slip of the tongue or whether he really didn't know what he was talking about, what he was saying would, in fact, choke off the economy, not stimulate it. Problem is, if you aren't an economist, would you know that he screwed it up? Probably not.

So I'm going to be the guy that calls B.S. on the B.S. Which is sometimes exactly what the financial journalists tell you.

This very matter about predictions for 2012, let's put that into its proper place. Will 2012 be a good year or not?

As a matter of fact, I can answer that question with complete certainty. Just ask me in a year's time.

Until then, it's anyone's guess what happens in the short term. And I really do mean guess.

I like to listen to sports radio. Recently I had the radio on, and one of the experts was doing his weekly predictions for the upcoming games.

Okay, here's what you need to know about this. This particular fellow is actually a former football player himself. He enjoyed a lengthy and successful career in the Canadian Football League. So he knows his football.

The other thing is that he isn't predicting the results of every football game. Just the ones that he feels the most confident about. These predictions were his weekly sure-fire, can't miss, go to Vegas and bet it big, guaranteed locks.

So, given that he knows the game, and that these predictions are the ones that he feels best about, you would think that our football expert would be fairly reliable in predicting the results, right?

Wrong. The expert's season record was 12 -15. And he was an expert. And these were this best picks. Could have done better flipping a coin.

You see, that's the thing about predictions for the future. They are inherently dubious.

Now, don't forsake all hope. Markets are remarkably predictable in the long run. It's just what happens from day to day that is a crapshoot.

So to sum this up, what we have is the melodramatic tendencies of financial journalists to make a big deal of mundane affairs, questions about the qualifications of these same financial journalists to provide insightful analysis, and the inherent unreliability about short-term predictions. Maybe the next time a financial journalist tells you how the next catastrophe is imminent you can put that type of comment in proper perspective.

One of the vital determinants of whether you are able to do the things that you really want to in life is to make financial decisions that are consistent with your objectives, and to not let yourself get distracted by the melodramatic pronouncements of financial journalists.

And that's no B.S.

From December 2011

Doomsday in 2012?

THIS IS THE TIME of the year where a bunch of people are going to tell you their best guess for the next 12 months. And that's exactly what it is. A guess. 2012 WILL BRING some more talk about the world coming to an end. The latest countdown to Armageddon comes courtesy of an ancient Mayan belief that the end of a 5,125 year cycle happens on December 21, 2012, bringing much catastrophe.

Of course, we don't have to go too far back for the last doomsday prediction. Just a few months ago the American religious figure Harold Camping was talking fire, brimstone and plague, culminating in the end of the world in October 2011. Previously, Camping had also predicted the end of days happening in May 1988 and again in September 1994.

Predictions that the world is ending are nothing new. 16th Century seer Nostradamus made a number of vague and ambiguous predictions that willing believers could twist into a description of real life events, but his most famous prediction was quite specific. In July 1999 the King of Terror was to descend from the sky.

These types of dire prognostications can cause quite a stir. But clearly, just because someone says something is going to happen doesn't mean that it actually will. Even if it's Nostradamus doing the saying.

Sooner or later you are going to see what some guy thinks is going to happen in the next 12 months or so. The only possible exception to this would be if you never watch the news, don't spend any time on the internet, never read your mutual fund or pension statement, and you don't read the newspaper.

The reason that I can pretty much guarantee you are eventually going to come across what some guy thinks is going to happen in the next 12 months or so is because that's the way the financial world is hard-wired. It's all about what's happening now, about anticipating tomorrow, about getting out in front of what's going on.

This penchant for predictions is so pervasive that I even saw a recent article where a guy was making his annual economic forecast using one of those Magic 8-Balls, made in China by Mattel. Obviously he's writing tongue-in-cheek here, but last year the 8-Ball ended up beating many of the financial gurus in predicting oil prices, gold prices, inflation, and the pace of the economic recovery.

There are two things that a reader can take from the 8-Ball predictions. If a novelty toy can beat the financial gurus then clearly a person doesn't need to put much faith in the predictions of these financial gurus. The second, horrifying thing is that someone out there somewhere really is going to be making financial decisions based on the predictions of the Magic 8-Ball.

The perverse and grotesque reality of all this is that what happens in the next 12 months rarely matters in the long-term. I know it sounds counter-intuitive, but that's the truth.

This market timing and stock selection cult that has evolved is something akin to a bunch of schoolboys feverishly combing the playground to see who can find the largest ant. Even if you end up finding the largest ant on the planet, it's still an insect, and insects are small.

The dominant factor that determines your investment results is not what mutual fund you buy, nor is it when you buy it. The dominant factor is your own investor behaviour.

Notice I didn't say *investment* behaviour. What I said was that the dominant factor that determines your investment results is your own *investor* behaviour. Investor behaviour refers to what you do when prices get cheap. It refers to what you do when prices get expensive. It refers to how much you save. It's about making decisions that are consistent with your financial objectives. And, make no mistake, investor behaviour is more important than all of the other factors put together.

Sure, market timing and investment selection has a role. But these things account for roughly 5 percent of your real-life returns. Frankly, if you get the 95 percent right, the residual 5 percent can look after itself. And yet it's the 5 percent that gets all the attention.

I don't care if all the kids on the playground are foaming at the mouth in their frenzied efforts. Quit trying to find the largest ant, and let's take a look at the things that really matter. And predictions for the next 12 months ain't it.

By the way, when asked if the Mayan calendar is correct in its prediction that the world will end on Dec. 21, 2012, the Magic 8-Ball responded, "My sources say no."

From January 2012

■■■■■■

The "Grass is Greener" Epidemic

THERE SEEMS TO BE a vague, but strong feeling of uneasiness that has become entrenched in the outlook of many Canadians. An uncomfortable sense that things aren't going as well as they could be. A syndrome that points to the grass being greener on the other side of the fence.

And it seems like this "grass is greener" syndrome has become near epidemic.

It's not just me that is seeing this either. One of my colleagues from Alberta recently mentioned a call that he received from one of his clients, frantic that she has lost thousands of dollars.

"Slow down," he says. "Take a deep breath. Tell me what's wrong." It turns out that she is talking only 2011 market volatility. Except once my buddy runs the numbers, she is really up a bit.

The thing is, although her accounts were actually up in 2011, it didn't feel that way to her. To her, things felt ominous.

And she is far from alone. A recent poll showed an astounding 70 percent of Canadians think that the country is in a recession right now. We aren't, of course. The recession has been over for 30 months. But it doesn't feel that way, does it?

I saw an article recently that is typical of the type of thinking that is the fuel that feeds this unsettled impression of discomfort.

The title of the article was "Buffett no match for flat S&P500". Buffett, of course, is Warren Buffett, the world's greatest investor. Geez, if Buffett is struggling it's no wonder things are so tough for us mere mortals, eh?

The article then goes on to state "Buffett's Berkshire Hathaway Inc. slipped 4.7% in 2011. It was the second time since 1990 that the Omaha,

Nebraska-based firm underperformed an S&P 500 that had either declined for the year or rose less than 5%. Berkshire gained about 17-fold in the 21-year period, while the index has nearly quadrupled."

Okay, just in case this is a little too subtle, I'm going to draw specific attention to it. The headline is "Buffett no match for flat S&P500". And then the author proceeds to state *in the same article* how such circumstances have only arisen twice in 21 years, and over that time Berkshire Hathaway shares have gone up *seventeen times* versus the S&P up four times.

What kind of a planet do we live on that a guy can outperform by that much, and still have that headline written? It's like scoring a hat trick to win game seven of the Stanley Cup finals, and the reporter wants to ask you about that goal post you hit back in the second period.

The problem with the grass-is-greener syndrome is that it has people doing things that they really shouldn't be doing. It has people scrapping perfectly acceptable investments that are consistent with their financial objectives because they think that they should be doing better. Just exactly how it is that they should be doing better is usually not clearly defined, just that there is this perception that they should be.

Recently I received an email from a person who owns a Group Retirement Savings Plan with another firm. She said "What's the deal with the stock markets? My latest statement I put in almost 1000 bucks yet my portfolio value from last month ended up down by a couple hundred....please reassure me that I've got them buying into the right funds."

To which I immediately replied, "Give me a break. Put your money in, keep your money in, be happy when things go down so you can buy more shares with your $1000."

But I was also interested in where she was coming from, so I picked up the phone and gave her a call.

I explained that I had two purposes. One was to reassure her, since she really is doing just fine. But the other thing was to explore why she felt the way she did.

I asked her what it was that is the reason for her concern. She said "It looks like I am losing money month after month after month." See, that's interesting to me. Because she is, in fact, not losing money month after month.

Actually she is doing quite well. But she gets one bad statement in the mail and, in an instant, all recollection of her previous impressive gains has vanished completely, replaced by the bitterness and woe associated with the most recent 90-day period.

Her impression is that she is losing money. She's frustrated. But her impression differs from reality. She isn't losing money.

I asked her, "What if I sent you a two-page article? Would you read that?" Nope, she doesn't have the time.

She doesn't have the time to read two pages to become a better educated investor. She's scared and frustrated and confused, but she doesn't have five minutes to become better informed.

I ask her how much it is that she thinks she has lost. She figures that she has lost around 20 percent of her holdings. No wonder she is frustrated. But she is wrong, she hasn't lost anything. It just *feels* to her that she has lost twenty percent. That didn't actually happen.

Now, this an interesting part. She says "I know that in the future the markets will go up. I'm not planning on retiring anytime soon."

Okay, so why is it that you need reassurance then?

I told her of my trip to the grocery store the previous night. Much to my pleasure, I found my favourite type of fruit & veggie juice on sale. So I bought an armload. When you get a chance to buy a quality product at a cheap price you should embrace that opportunity.

That's the way that she should be looking at her investments. When the markets go down she should be excited, because now her monthly purchase allows her to buy even more shares in Coca Cola and Berkshire Hathaway and Disney and Apple and Royal Bank and Canadian Natural Resources and McDonalds and a couple hundred additional businesses of similar pedigree.

When prices are cheap she gets more shares for her monthly investment. She wants cheap prices to buy investments, just as I want cheap prices to buy my fruit & veggie drink.

Finally we had a breakthrough. She realized that she was looking at the wrong column on her statement.

Instead of looking at the market value, which is a temporary snapshot of what her accounts were worth at a moment in time that has already passed, she should be looking at the number of shares that she has. Even more, she should find delight in the increasing number of shares that she owns, because that is what is going to determine her eventual wealth.

The market value on her past statement is simply what her investments used to be worth. But the number of shares that she owns is her claim to participate in the growth and prosperity of a diversified collection of world-class businesses. The more shares that she acquires, the more wealth she will have. It's as easy as that.

So let's talk about this grass-is-greener syndrome. Are you scrapping perfectly acceptable investments that are consistent with your financial objectives because you have a vague, yet unsubstantiated, perception that you could be doing better?

Or are you taking the time to become a more educated investor? Are you taking advantage of cheap prices when opportunity presents itself and buying more shares of quality investments?

Because if you want your grass to look a little greener you are going to need to water it from time to time.

From January 2012

■ ■ ■ ■ ■ ■

Reversion to the Mean

LAST WEEK I TOOK A PHONE CALL from a "wholesaler." Wholesalers are my main point of contact with mutual fund companies, and they can be great resources. But, make no mistake; the reason that wholesalers call me is because they want me to sell their products. There is no free lunch.

This phone call was no different. The wholesaler offered me some client-friendly material on tax planning, which I gladly accepted. But he also offered to share some information on his fixed income products. I'm not interested in that at all, but lots of people are. Right now, those products are very popular, as people look to avoid the variability of the equity markets.

The wholesaler says something along the lines of having a good option for people looking to avoid uncertain markets, and enquires if that is the type of solution that I am looking for at the moment.

"Not even remotely", I say. "On the contrary, I think that this is the time to buy equities, not fixed income." And, perhaps just to shock the guy a little, I add "And, in particular, US equities interest me greatly."

The USA, of course, is currently subject to all kinds of fear-mongering about its imminent demise. So basically what I have just told him is that I am rejecting his most-popular option, and would rather look at his most-unloved option. You see, when it comes to investments, there are investments that are easy to sell, and then there are investments that people should be buying, and usually the groups are mutually exclusive.

I tell the wholesaler that I am a contrarian. Unlike most people, I don't want to buy what has already done well. I want to buy what will do well next.

"Ah", he says. "The US. Lots of beaten up companies down there."

"Nope", I say. "Lots of wonderful companies trading at beaten-up prices." Which is not at all the same thing as buying beaten-up companies.

And that's a true story. US corporations are a who's-who of business success stories. And they are more profitable than ever. And they are sitting on mountains of cash. And nobody wants them. Which means I can buy these wonderful companies at incredibly attractive prices.

Meanwhile, there is the popular fixed income option. Think about the name for a moment. Fixed income. Do you really want to live on a fixed income? In a rising-cost world? Probably not. Yet fixed income products are all the rage. That makes no sense, but there you are.

Then you have companies like Apple. Apple just made 17.5 billion dollars. In the last quarter. And these are the types of businesses that people are avoiding? That also makes no sense, but there you are.

Folks, let me tell you about something called "reversion to the mean". Basically what it means is that if the short-term results have drifted away from the long-term averages, sooner or later you are going to see things get back in synch. In other words, investments that are currently in vogue, such as fixed income, do not outperform forever. And quality investments that are currently lagging, such as US equities, do not underperform forever.

Here's an example about long-term averages. Prior to the 2008 financial meltdown, the long-term average for the Toronto Stock Exchange was 10.5 percent. After 2008, a year in which the TSX declined by about 40 percent, the long-term average was 10.1 percent. In other words, even though there was a big one year swing, the long-term average return barely budged. Returns might be unpredictable in the short-term, but they are remarkably stable in the long run.

So if you have an asset class that has an extended period of performance below its long-term averages, it most probably means that you are going to see an extended period of outperformance to get back to the long-term performance number.

And what has the last decade been if not an extended period of underperformance for the equity markets?

Reversion to the mean. As Gretzky said when asked what makes him great – don't skate to where the puck is. Skate to where it's going to be.

From February 2012

Fees: First Things First

LATELY I HAVE HEARD of a number of conversations that have had a similar theme. Unfortunately, the common sense that sparked the conversation has been, in many cases, obliterated by a dogmatic pursuit of something that seems like a good idea – seeking low fees on your investments.

I'm in no way advocating for high fees, but the whole idea of fees on your investments really is getting too much attention relative to more important matters.

And often it's undeservedly so. If your mutual funds happened to go down by ten percent, it wasn't merely the fees that caused that. It was the markets.

If the market is off by ten percent, then similar mutual funds went down too. It's just a question of whether they went down by 9.8% or 10.2%. Fees cause incremental changes to your results, they don't drive your results.

Sure, incremental results are worth paying attention to, but the more important issue by far is owning the right investments in the first place, combined with your own behaviour as an investor. Get that right and you now have the luxury of trying to seek incremental improvements. Botch that one, however, and the effect of fees on your portfolio is drowned out by far more impactful forces.

Still, all things being equal cheap fees are better than expensive ones. At the end of the day the less that you pay in fees the more that is left for you.

But the problem with blindly accepting the dogma that cheap equals better is that you stop thinking about stuff. The question of fees on your investments is a legitimate question, but it's a question that can put you in a treacherous situation.

Here's the deal. All things being equal, it is wise and good to seek to reduce your fees. But the absolutely critical part is the part about all things being equal.

For instance, let's say that you are looking for a Canadian Dividend fund and you are comparing Dividend Fund A to Dividend Fund B. The top holdings of the respective funds are highly correlated, but fund A comes with a Management Expense Ratio (the annual fee for owning mutual funds) of 1.56%, while Fund B has a Management Expense Ratio of 2.87%. In that case, the less expensive investment, all things being equal, is quite likely to be the preferred option.

You'll want to compare the all-in costs of your various options though. Mutual fund management fees are one cost, but they aren't the only cost that investors can be exposed to. If your mutual fund cost $80 per year to own, and an exchange traded fund with a similar mandate costs $8 per year to own, but the administration fee on the brokerage account needed to hold the ETF is $100 annually, how much money have you saved?

So it's fine to compare the total cost of similar products, but the problem is that if you start favouring bonds or GICs over equity funds based purely on price. That is not a logical comparison. You are comparing the price of two different things. It would be like saying a box of crayons is less expensive than a choice cut of steak.

Would you make that decision based purely on price? Of course not. I don't really care how cheap the crayons are if I am hungry, and I wouldn't care about the fine quality of the steak if I was a vegetarian.

For decisions like this the primary deciding factor is what it is that you are trying to do. Are you needing supplies for art class or for a backyard BBQ? Having first determined what you need, now is the appropriate time to look at price. But first you have to determine your needs.

Back in July, I happened by a sign that said "Closing Out Sale, Everything 60% Off". As it turned out I had just blown out my pair of sandals and the thought of cruising the hot summer beaches wearing black motorcycle boots was not appealing, so off I went to seek out some new sandals.

I was a little late to the party, however. I'm a size ten, but there was not a single pair of men's footwear larger than a size nine. No sandals, no sneakers, no golf shoes, no hip waders. Nothing.

So what did I do? Did I buy a pair of shoes that didn't fit just because they were cheap? Of course not.

They did, however, have some kid's bikes on sale, and my kids needed bikes.

The bikes were cheap, I wanted them for my kids, so I bought them on the spot, even though that meant packing them around for the rest of my vacation before hauling them home.

The bikes are perfect. Emily is five, and she got a new Tinkerbell bike with flashing lights and sound effects. William is three, and he got a flashy new Spiderman bike with training wheels. They love them.

Here's one more thing for consideration, though. While the bikes were of good quality and available at a great price, I wouldn't buy one for myself. I couldn't ride them – I wouldn't even want to try – they are kid's bikes; far too small for a grown man. What is a good fit for one person is not necessarily a good fit for all people, and that has nothing to do with price.

There isn't a week that goes by when someone asks me a question in which I reply "It depends on your objectives." Should I top up my retirement savings plan? Should I buy or should I rent? Should I get a term insurance policy or a permanent insurance policy? It all depends on your objectives.

Always keep your objectives in mind. Having first determined what products will meet your objectives, you can then look for the best price. But looking at price first means you might be trying to cram your size ten feet into size nine shoes, and you would look pretty funny pedaling down the street riding a Spiderman bike with training wheels.

In fact, your objective is not even going to be simply to have the lowest cost portfolio. Your objective is going to be something along the lines of being able to retire when you want, with the lifestyle you want and to be able to maintain that lifestyle for the duration of your lifetime. Alternatively, it could be seeing your kids through post-secondary education without hanging the albatross of a six-digit student loan around their neck. Or it might even be to be able to be there for your aged parents when their health starts to fade. Those are real objectives. Keeping costs down is one component of reaching your objectives, but it isn't an objective in itself.

You want to be cheap? Sometimes that can be a case of be careful what you ask for. If the product is a bad fit, and it doesn't move you closer to your objectives, then it doesn't matter what the price is.

First things first. Figure out what your objectives are, determine what types of products are consistent with your objectives, and then – and only then – is it appropriate to look for ways to bring your costs down.

From August 2012

Long-Term Investing Is Alive and Well

RECENTLY THERE WAS AN ARTICLE that ran in an industry publication that was titled "Long-Term Investing is Dead." It contained a logical and well-reasoned argument with supporting evidence, and the conclusion was "the bottom line for investors is that they can no longer have a long-term investment horizon, which is widely considered the key to success."

It compelled me to write to the publication. My response was, "Ridiculous. Of course long-term investing isn't dead. Quit trying to be a tabloid."

Long-term investing is far from dead. Indeed, long-term investing is the only type of investing there is. If you have a short time frame you can be a saver, or you are a speculator, but you aren't an investor.

When I was invited to write a rebuttal for the same publication, the editor offered me the materials from the presentation that the original article was drawn from. I said that I don't need those materials. You see, I categorically reject these types of Doomsday predictions for the future for the simple reasons that they are inherently unreliable and often horribly inaccurate.

That goes for any prediction of the future, not just for investments. Before last year's Stanley Cup playoffs began, the consensus expert prediction was that the Vancouver Canucks and Pittsburgh Penguins would face off in the Finals. And these predictions weren't just from casual hockey fans; this is what the guys who make their living analyzing the sport were saying. A lot of good those predictions were. Both the Canucks and the Penguins were bounced in the first round.

The financial world is obsessed with trying to predict the future. But the collective track record of these wannabe soothsayers is unadulteratedly abysmal. As Peter Lynch famously stated, "Every year I talk to the executives of a thousand companies, and I can't avoid hearing from the various gold bugs, interest-rate disciples, Federal Reserve watchers, and fiscal mystics quoted in the newspapers. Thousands of experts study overbought indicators, oversold indicators, head-and-shoulder patterns, put-call ratios, the Fed's policy on money supply, foreign investment, the movement of the constellations through the heavens, and the moss on oak trees, and they can't predict markets with any useful consistency, any more than the gizzard squeezers could tell the Roman emperors when the Huns would attack.".

This is far from the first time someone has claimed that this time it's different. Whenever I see a story like "Long-Term Investing is Dead" I think back to the infamous cover story that ran in BusinessWeek magazine titled "The Death of Equities." This was another logical and well-reasoned argument with supporting evidence, and the conclusion was "the old attitude of buying solid stocks as a cornerstone for one's life savings and retirement has simply disappeared."

The thing is, this "Death of Equities" article, which claims systematic and insurmountable mega-problems will push the planet's economies over the precipice to certain destruction, was written in 1979, the inception of the greatest bull market in history. It's actually one of the worst market calls ever made. Go read "The Death of Equities" and then compare the real market results from then until now. It will put the "Long-Term Investing is Dead" article in proper perspective. This time is not different. It never is.

So does the world have challenges? Of course it does. But, amazingly, people continuously forget that it is these very challenges that present opportunities.

We would be well served to keep Warren Buffett's hamburger quiz in mind:

"A short quiz: If you plan to eat hamburgers throughout your life and are not a cattle producer, should you wish for higher or lower prices for beef? Likewise, if you are going to buy a car from time to time but are not an auto manufacturer, should you prefer higher or lower car prices? These questions, of course, answer themselves."

"But now for the final exam: If you expect to be a net saver during the next five years, should you hope for a higher or lower stock market during that period?"

"Many investors get this one wrong. Even though they are going to be net buyers of stocks for many years to come, they are elated when stock prices rise and depressed when they fall. In effect, they rejoice because prices have risen for the "hamburgers" they will soon be buying."

"This reaction makes no sense. Only those who will be sellers of equities in the near future should be happy at seeing stocks rise. Prospective purchasers should much prefer sinking prices."

The future is intrinsically unpredictable. Accept that, and focus on making smart decisions with their money, consistent with their financial objectives. Do that and predictions about what happens in the next five minutes are not material.

The plain, pure truth is that pretending that you can forecast the future, or time the markets, or even fully comprehend the swirling confluence of innumerable variables, including animal spirits, and summarize it all in a few short sound bites is self-deceptive behaviour.

The "Long-Term Investing is Dead" story can just fade away, unremembered and unmourned. As a lifelong Canucks fan still smarting from their humbling early exit from the playoffs, I can tell you that's the proper place for predictions of the future.

From August 2012

■■■■■■

Making a Big Deal Out of Everything

IT'S THE NIGHT BEFORE the U.S. Presidential election, and I'm tired of people crying wolf every time they see a shadow. For example, lately President Obama has been taking some heat over an 8% unemployment rate.

This is not the first time a Democratic president has been criticized about the number of people out of work. John F. Kennedy took a lot of flack over the unemployment rate 50 years ago.

Guess what the unemployment rate was back then? Yep, 8%.

That's right. Far from this being some unknown economic territory, the current U.S. unemployment rate is pretty much exactly the same as it was 50 years ago.

You want to know what Kennedy called an 8% unemployment rate? 92% employment.

Meanwhile, let's look at what life was like during the Kennedy administration.

Kennedy is remembered for a lot of things. The thing I always think of first when I think of Kennedy is the Cuban Missile Crisis.

In 1962 Kennedy went eyeball to eyeball with Nikita Khrushchev over the establishment of nuclear missile bases in Cuba, 90 miles away from the United States mainland. This would have given Russia the ability to launch a nuclear first strike, and it put every major US city in the continental US with the exception of Seattle within range.

What people sometimes forget is that Kennedy already had Russia blanketed by nuclear threat, from bases in Europe and Turkey, and from the nuclear submarines that could be anywhere at any time. Khrushchev had problems of his own to worry about.

The result was a 13 day game of chicken between two nuclear superpowers, with the backdrop of the Cold War, for the highest stakes imaginable. If anyone blinked the consequence was mutually assured destruction, and the deaths of millions of people.

Nowadays if you try to fly into the United States with a nail file you'll get it confiscated. As far as threats go, it just does not compare.

You want to worry about something? Nuclear annihilation, now that's something worth getting freaked out about. It puts $4 a gallon gas into perspective, doesn't it?

Back home, Kennedy had to deal with racial tensions that could quickly turn violent. When peaceful civil rights demonstrators, including children, marched in Alabama they were met with fire hoses and trained dogs. It wasn't hooded members of the Klu Klux Klan that squared off with them either. It was policemen and firemen.

James Meredith was the first black student to attend the University of Mississippi. He was not made welcome. But it wasn't some local hot-heads that had a problem. It was the Governor of Mississippi that personally tried blocking Meredith's admittance.

Kennedy had to bring the armed troops to restore peace and order after people died in violent confrontation. These are not troops being shipped offshore to fight foreigners. These are American soldiers brought in to keep Americans from killing other Americans on American soil.

And Meredith wasn't just some high school kid. He'd already served his country for nine years in the US Air Force. That's what race relations was like in the Southern US in the 1960s.

Now think about all of the progress that has been made in the last 50 years.

Are there challenges out there today? Sure. Is an 8% unemployment rate the end of the world? Clearly not.

Yet the financial media and the pundits cry wolf. They cry wolf quite a lot, as a matter of fact.

This is somewhat of a recurring theme in the essays I write; the almost universal tendency of the financial media to report even banal events in over-the-top dramatic fashion.

You can probably tell this already, but I'm not really a writer. I've been doing these essays for fourteen years, but my degree is in economics, not journalism. So recently I asked one my friends, who is a real journalist, if this sort of thing was taught in journalism school; the same formulaic headlines repeated over and over again, the continual pronouncement that whatever is the crisis of the day as the probable beginning of the end.

Clearly journalists write with purpose, and I was wondering, if this is something that was formally learned. So I asked her whether scaring the crap out of people is something that is actually taught in journalism school. And I was completely serious in the asking of my question.

Separately, another friend – this one happens to be in the investment industry – recently shared a story of someone he met that is paying 1.2% annually for financial advice, yet she has no idea how she's doing versus relevant benchmark.

My comment to him was that was the wrong question to be asking. The right question to ask is whether she is going to achieve her objectives. Benchmarks are for pundits, goals are for clients.

His reply was that punditry is still essential. But is it?

Think about this for a moment. If the client reaches her goals in keeping with her risk tolerance, but she trails the "benchmark" (whatever that is), did she lose? If benchmark is up 30%, but she is only up 25%, is she sad?

On the other hand, if she beats the "benchmark" (again, whatever that means), but she doesn't meet her objectives, did she win? If the benchmark goes down by 30%, but she is only down by 25%, is she happy?

This focus on benchmarks is not only silly, it is potentially dangerous if it takes the focus off why a person is investing in first place. Call me thick if you want, but I continue to fail to grasp why we have all these people comparing investment performance to some hypothetical measuring stick that has no direct relation to their own personal success or failure.

Anyway, I guess what I am trying to say is this. Folks, not everything is a big deal. Real life is not like the way it gets portrayed on television. You don't need to get all worked up about every little flight of fancy.

Not all problems are big. Even big problems are surmountable. If you want to achieve your goals then get yourself a good plan, stick to the plan, and don't get distracted by people crying wolf every time they see a shadow.

From November 2012

■ ■ ■ ■ ■ ■

Invest With Purpose

RECENTLY I BECAME FAMILIAR with a situation that seems to defy rational explanation.

A person owned some mutual funds that were selected by an advisor. These mutual funds were appropriate for the client's long-term objectives.

The client also owned some stocks. These stocks were a couple of junior oil and gas stocks, and they were selected by the client. The advisor was merely acting as an order taker for the stock purchase.

A couple of years go by. The mutual funds are up by a few dollars. The short-term returns on these long-term investments would be in the single digits. The returns are positive, but nobody is bragging too much. This performance is consistent with similar investments, however. Over this particular time period, the mutual fund returns are more a function of the market conditions than the specific product.

The stocks, on the other hand, are down by about 40 percent.

So, to summarize: The mutual funds, which were purchased with the objective of achieving a long-term financial objective, are consistent with the client's declared objectives and risk tolerance, and are performing in line with comparable products, were selected by the financial advisor. The stocks, which have wet the bed, were selected by the client.

So now that we are a few dozen months into a long term plan, guess what happens? The client sells the mutual funds and keeps the stocks.

There are a number of aspects to this that make it fascinating.

Why would the client sell a diversified portfolio of professionally managed investments that has competitive performance, while simultaneously keeping the amateurly selected stinkers? After all, what is the mutual fund but simply a collection of stocks? So why sell a diversified collection of stocks that are professionally managed, but keep the ones that were self-selected?

It is possible that the client wants to keep the stocks because he has some sort of attachment to them. Maybe he actually knows the company very well, and is comfortable with its prospects for the future. As reasons go, this is a good one.

But, although it is possible that he knows the company very well, it is far more common that he is making one or more amateur's mistakes.

It could be that he doesn't want to sell the stocks because that would be tantamount to confessing he made a mistake on the purchase, and who likes admitting they made a mistake?

It could be that he is fixated on the price that he paid for them, and intends to sell "once the stock recovers". The problem with that is the stock doesn't know what price he paid for it, and the stock doesn't care what price he paid for it. In other words, this really just comes down to pure blind hope that the stock will recover in price, with no rational framework to base that recovery on.

It could be that he assigns more trust and faith to whatever it was that he relied on to make the stock purchase than he does to the skills of his advisor and the professional money manager running the mutual fund. That occasionally might be appropriate but, more often than not, amateurs do not select stocks based on extensive research. They buy them for whimsical reasons, and whimsy is not a very good approach for making informed decisions.

Why would the client even be evaluating a long-term portfolio on a short-term basis in the first place?

Why would the client sell the mutual funds? It's not relative performance; the funds are performing fine relative to their peer group. It could be pure impatience based on the unrealistic expectation that long term results happen instantaneously.

And what is the client thinking that he is going to do next with the proceeds of the liquidated mutual fund?

It could be that he is looking at his stock-based portfolio and comparing it to a fixed-income strategy. That's nuts, but it's happening all the time. It's the equivalent of finding a week during which Hawaii experienced inclement weather at the same time that Fort St. John, British Columbia saw some sun, and from that extrapolating that northern Canada must have a better climate than Hawaii.

What people need to understand about fixed income investing is that the glory days are behind us. Nowadays the yields are ultra-low, but it gets worse. Build taxes and inflation into the equation, and these products have negative real returns, with no meaningful prospects for doing much better.

People who are scared off the equity investing by variable returns and instead putting their money into fixed income investments are behaving like the old story of the ostrich that sticks his head in sand, thinking if he can't see the danger he is safe.

Inflation is the danger that you can't see. Don't be an ostrich, and equate pretending risk isn't there as being the same thing as protecting yourself against risk.

I can't say for sure why the client did what he did. The bottom line is that you should make your financial decisions with good reason. Fear, greed, whimsy, and impatience really are not reasons; they are merely how you justify your impulses. Don't be impulsive. Invest with purpose.

From December 2012

■ ■ ■ ■ ■ ■

It All Depends

LET'S CALL A SPADE A SPADE. I am a messy guy.

Here's how bad the mess can get. Molly Maid cleans my office, and I am going to hire them to clean my house too. But before I have them start, I need to tidy up a bit. Think about that for a moment. I need to clean my house before I let the maid service commence with cleaning my house.

Given that, I'm sure that you can picture that my truck is a mess too. There are a couple of contributing factors. With winter everything is gucky, of course. Slushy snow on the floor mats, road grime on the exterior. But also my kids are ages 4 and 6, so you just know the backseat is full of toys, wrappers and single mittens.

So is this clutter in my truck a big deal? Well, it all depends.

If I was going to enter my truck in a show-and-shine competition, then yes, the mess is a big deal. But winning a show-and-shine is not my objective.

There are other things about my truck that are far more important to me. Safe, comfortable and reliable transportation for myself and my family. The ability to navigate in our northern climate. Being able to haul water for the horses without getting stuck in a snowy pasture. Reasonable operating expenses. These are the things that I care about.

Now that you know all this about me, should I sell my truck, merely because it is dirty? After all, if the truck isn't perfect, one option is to simply get rid of it. Perhaps not a wise option, but it is an option.

The thing about it is, the messy part of the truck is what you see. It's harder to see the safety and reliability. The mess is in your face, demanding attention. And if you let it, the mess can be a distraction from what is actually important.

The purpose of this little anecdote is to draw the distinction between options, distractions, and objectives.

I do have some options with what to do about my messy truck. Obviously, selling a truck purely because it is a little dirty is just silly. In other circumstances, however, the silly options can be harder to identify.

For me, having a messy truck is merely a distraction. Clearly, if having clean truck was more important to me I'd simply clean my truck. In other circumstances, however, the distractions from what is truly important can also be harder to identify.

So, in a world with an overwhelming amount of options, and with innumerable distractions, how does a person make good decisions?

The process is actually very simple. Don't focus on the all of the things that you can possibly do; these are your options and you can be paralyzed into inaction by information overload. Don't focus on all the reasons why you shouldn't do something; these are often the distractions, and can take your focus off of what is truly important.

Instead, focus on what you want to accomplish. As Steven Covey says, "Begin with the end in mind."

You see, if you understand what it is that you are trying to accomplish, then you can quickly screen out all of the things that are not consistent with your objectives, and make good, informed decisions that move you closer to whatever it is that you are trying to do.

Here's a practical example. I was talking to my buddy recently. He had some questions about what he should do with a couple of extra bucks he has kicking around.

His current retirement savings plans are invested for growth, so he's thinking that he should have some low risk investments to balance things out. He doesn't have a Tax Free Savings Account set up yet. That's nagging at him a bit; he'd like to get a Tax Free Savings Account established. He sees the local bank branch is advertising 2.25% interest for TFSA investments, which seems like a decent interest rate. So what should he do?

My response to him was, "Bottom line – it all depends on what you are looking to accomplish." And then we stopped talking about products, and started talking about what it was that he wanted to do.

See, here's the thing. I love Tax Free Savings Accounts. They are a fantastic vehicle for both saving and for investment. And the 2.25% bank offering is probably a decent product, for what it does.

But none of those things are consistent with the client's objectives.

He's thinking about using this money for his retirement, and that's three decades from now. He has very high income, so he has the corresponding tax problem. He doesn't need liquidity, he doesn't need income. He has a long time frame and a decent tolerance for variability in his returns.

Now, what we could have done is compare the 2.25% that the bank is paying to similar products. We could also have compared the 2.25% to products that are quite different.

But rather than comparing products, what we did was look at what it is that my friend wanted to do. When you do that, it is clear that the fixed rate TFSA doesn't fit him at all.

He has options, and there are always distractions. But when we clarify his objectives, the appropriate decision becomes an easy one to make. You simply do the things that move you closer to where you want to be, and there is nothing about this particular TFSA option that helps this particular client meet his specific objectives.

What should you do with your money? It all depends on what you want to accomplish.

Don't ask, "What can I do?" Instead, ask, "What should I do to reach my objectives?"

From January 2013

It's Not What You Make;
It's What You Do With It

HAVE YOU HEARD the expression "Big hat, no cattle"? It means sometimes a showy display of wealth can be misleading.

Thomas Stanley and William Danko have carefully documented the study of wealth in their book "The Millionaire Next Door". During their research they held a focus group interview and dinner for ten first-generation millionaires.

At the dinner a vice president of a trust department, a man who wears a $5000 watch and drives a current model luxury imported car, remarked "These people can't be millionaires! They don't look like millionaires, they don't dress like millionaires, they don't act like millionaires – they don't even have millionaire names. Where are the millionaires who look like millionaires?"

If you were to ask the average person what a millionaire looks like most people would opt for the trust officer – the man with the $5000 watch. But looks can be deceiving.

So how do these people, who are typically in businesses classified as "dull-normal", end up doing so well? The big secret is that it is not what they make; it's what they do with it that counts.

To illustrate the idea that it's not what you make, but rather what you do with it that determines success, let's look our national springtime fascination... the Stanley Cup Playoffs!

The New York Rangers, a team with a $68 million payroll, misses the playoffs. The defending Stanley Cup Champions Detroit Red Wings, a team with a $67 million payroll, is swept in the first round by the upstart Anaheim

Mighty Ducks. The Colorado Avalanche, with a $60 million payroll, is eliminated in the first round by the unheralded Minnesota Wild. The St. Louis Blues, with their $63 million payroll, went out in the first round to the Vancouver Canucks. The Dallas Stars, with their $61 million payroll, made it to the second round, but then Anaheim took them out as well.

Back to the Millionaire Next Door. About 95 percent of American millionaires have a net worth between $1 million and $10 million. Stanley and Danko focus their book on this segment for good reason – this level of wealth can be achieved in one generation.

So how does one achieve such success? Stanley and Danko found that millionaires live well below their means. They wear inexpensive suits, and they don't drive the newest, fanciest car. They spend only about 7 percent of their total wealth each year.

They are fastidious investors. On average they invest nearly 20 percent of their annual household income. Most invest at least 15 percent of their income each year. They hold nearly 20 percent of their wealth in stocks or mutual funds, but they rarely sell their equity investments.

These millionaires aren't celebrities, or athletes, or lottery winners, or recipients of large inheritances. Literally, they are the guy next door. They have six and a half times the wealth of their non-millionaire neighbours, who typically trade wealth to acquire high-status material possessions.

Stanley and Danko give a formula to determine how much your net worth should be, whatever your age or income. Multiply your age times your realized pre-tax annual household income from all sources except inheritances. Divide by ten. This, less any inherited wealth, is what your net worth should be.

From May 2011

■■■■■■

Brad Brain has a Crystal Ball

On October 18, 2000 both the Dow Jones and the TSE 300 closed below 10,000, which put them back roughly to where they were a year ago. As I write this the TSE 300 has sunk lower yet.

Was this unexpected? Far from it. Here are some excerpts from some of my past essays.

"For anyone who has exposure to the real high-octane stuff, imagine the next investment statement you receive is worth half as much as your last statement. If you have a hard time with this, it is time to examine your portfolio.

Know your investment; know what you own and why you own it. Know the risks involved, and know what to do when we see the inevitable next round of market volatility." March 13, 2000

"The mania for technology is not about the world as it exists today. It's about potential, and what these companies might do in the future. Well, there is a mammoth difference between what might happen, and what actually happens.

With every major advance in society there comes a flood of investment capital. And most of the initial capital is eventually lost. I am not talking about an investment going down; I am talking about it going away completely." March 27, 2000

"This is danger here. Some people are shelling out big bucks for companies that are losing money based on expectations that these companies will grow into successful enterprises. The danger lies in that if we have some sort of wakeup call – perhaps an interest rate hike, or a company missing its forecasted earnings – market sentiment will turn from greed to fear, and there will be a stampede for the exits.

The implication of all of this is that we are likely to see continued stock market volatility, and we may very well see a substantial market decline of twenty percent, or more." July 24, 2000

Who is this Brad Brain, Certified Financial Planner? And where did he get a crystal ball? How could he have so accurately predicted the big market swoon in late October?

Confession time, folks. It ain't all that hard to predict a market meltdown after a sustained period of unsustainable growth. It was only a matter of time.

The tricky question is not "if" the markets drop. It is a matter of certainty that they eventually will. The tricky question is "when" they will drop. And that, my friends, is completely unknowable. No person that has ever walked the face of this earth has been able to accurately predict with any degree of reliability the fickle moves of Mr. Market. So don't try it. Just say no to market timing.

Will the markets bounce right back? Maybe. Will they get even cheaper? Could happen. When will they recover? Nobody knows. Will they recover? Without any doubt or hesitation, I say yes they will.

One thing is for sure, right now you can accumulate shares in wonderful businesses and you can do it for cheaper than it would have cost you last week. And that makes a world of sense if you are a long-term investor.

Here's a final blast from the past:

"If you are a true investor you relish the opportunity to pick up shares in world class companies at bargain prices. Every once in a while the stock market has a big sale. Speculators call these events crashes, corrections, or adjustments. Investors call them opportunities."

From October 2000

■ ■ ■ ■ ■ ■

What I Believe

THERE ARE MANY THEORIES on how to create and preserve wealth. Some of these theories can be quite effective. At least for a while. But when it comes right down to it, there is only one methodology that I have full faith in – Value Investing.

In simple terms, value investing involves determining the intrinsic value of an enterprise, and then buying the investment at a discount to its true worth. We are looking for good businesses at good prices, and we are not willing to compromise on either aspect. From this simple definition several principles arise:

Principle number one: Own great businesses. If a business is doing well and is managed by people with integrity, intelligence and energy, its inherent value will ultimately be reflected in its share price.

Principle number two: Build concentrated portfolios. Many investors are over-diversified. This leads to a dilution of the quality of investments, with too much capital tied up in poor investments and not enough in the really good ones. I prefer to find a fewer number of great investment ideas and to take meaningful positions rather than resorting to second or third-best ideas. Approximately 25 businesses are adequate to give diversification to a properly constructed portfolio. Adding more than that does not materially increase the benefits of diversification, but it does increase the detrimental dilution factor.

Principle number three: Invest in what you know. Some investors will make an investment without really understanding why they would want to invest in a business, or even just what it is that they are investing into in the first place. This is folly. I want to know a business inside and out. It is knowledge that allows us to avoid risk.

Principle number four: Ignore the stock market. Investment decisions should reflect an opinion of the long-term prospects for a business, not the short-term prospects for the stock market. The stock market is a tool that can be used for our advantage, it is not the arbiter of our client's well being. As Warren Buffett says, "As far as I am concerned, the stock market doesn't exist. It is only there as a reference to see if anyone is offering to do anything foolish."

Principle number five: Employ a margin of safety. The key to successful investing is the purchase of shares in good businesses when market prices are at a large discount to underlying business values for any variety of reasons. As Peter Cundill says, "I am looking to buy a dollar for fifty cents."

Principle number six: Be patient. Many of history's great investors have suggested that the key to their success lay not in what they did, but rather in what they did not do. They did not yield to their emotions or to the pressure to follow the crowd. Instead they focused on the businesses they owned and watched as their value compounded over time.

There are different ways that we can implement these ideas. We are always on the lookout for good ideas ourselves. We also team up with other like-minded professional investment managers.

The Great Warren Buffett said, "To invest successfully over a lifetime does not require a stratospheric IQ, unusual business insight, or inside information. What's required in a sound intellectual framework for making decisions, and the ability to keep emotions from corroding that framework."

These are the things that I believe in.

From March 2005

■ ■ ■ ■ ■ ■

It's a Sad Thing, but Not Everybody Loves Me

IN THE BUILD-UP to the War Between the States, the American senator Daniel Webster, in trying to keep the Union together and stave off civil war, said to his constituents "Necessity compels me to speak true rather than pleasant things. I should indeed like to please you; but I prefer to save you, whatever be your attitude towards me."

That quote resonates with me. In my professional life, I have Daniel Webster moments all the time. People sometimes want to hear platitudes, but I prefer to speak plainly.

Because of this habit of mine to speak plainly, another quote also resonates with me; this one from famed investor Charlie Munger: "It's a sad thing, but not everybody loves me."

Today I'm going to speak plainly about financial matters. Specifically, I'm going to speak about taking responsibility for your own behaviours. And, make no mistake; it's your own behaviour that is the transcendent factor in whether or not you are going to achieve your financial goals.

That's not a popular message. People don't want to hear about living within their means. People don't want to hear about making significant additions to their investments in the teeth of a bear market, when the TV personalities are babbling about the Four Horsemen of some kind of Financial Apocalypse. People don't want to hear about long-term perspective.

People want instant gratification. People want winning lottery tickets. People want the promise of high returns with no risk. People want short-cuts. People want hot stock tips. People can occasionally tolerate a bit of market volatility, as long as it's not too deep and doesn't last too long. People want a magic financial potion to make all their dreams come true.

Well, that might be what people want, and there are armies of sycophants salivating over the opportunity to pander to that. After all, giving people what they want is the easiest sale in the world.

But not me. Necessity compels me to speak true rather than pleasant things. I should indeed like to please you; but I prefer to save you, whatever be your attitude towards me.

There are no high returns without risk. There are no short-cuts. There are no magic financial potions.

Don't look for scapegoats. Don't blame the fraction of a percent differ-ence in the management fee of your mutual fund. Don't fear conspiracy the-ories of shadowy cabals rigging the game in order to ruthlessly exploit the naivety of the common man.

It's all about you and what you do.

Don't let this confound you; this is actually a liberating message. Because the implication is that the most important factors are completely within your own control.

What matters most as to whether you achieve your financial objectives is how much of your income you save and what you do when the markets go down. End of story.

In 2009 I was telling everyone who would listen, and many of those who wouldn't, that now was the time to invest. Why was I so passionate about getting money to work immediately? My passion was inversely proportionate to how much the markets came down in 2008. The cheaper things got, the more excited I got.

This is the antithesis of the mainstream financial media, who tend to say that the cheaper things get, then the worse the financial conditions of the day must be.

Some people listened to me; some people listened to the media. Let's see how that turned out.

Let's say for sake of discussion that you had investments of $100,000, the markets went down by 40% in 2008, and subsequently rebounded by 66%. For now let's not worry about exactly what it was that happened or who is to blame; those are things that you can't control. What you can control is what you did about it.

If you panicked and sold out in 2008 after the markets went down by 40%, then your $100,000 is now $60,000.

If you sat tight your $100,000 investment is worth $100,000 again, having fully recovered from the 2008 volatility.

If you put in another $100,000 at the end of 2008 you now have $266,000. The initial investment has fully recovered and the subsequent investment – the one that was made when investments were cheap to buy – turned out to be very lucrative.

The first person invested $100,000 and now has $60,000, losing 40 percent of their investment. The second person invested $100,000 and now has $100,000; they didn't lose a penny. The third person invested $200,000 and now has $266,000, making 33 percent on their money.

With such a range of potential outcomes stemming solely from investor behaviour, the impact of a fractional amount of fees paid on a mutual fund does not even register. And yet what we have is people wanting to engage in microscopic analysis of the stuff that is minorly important.

I think that, in no small part, the reason that people want to dwell on the stuff that is outside of their control is because it means that they can pretend that the stuff that is inside their control is not the issue.

I'm not saying that the stuff that is outside your control is inconsequential. What I'm saying is that just because some stuff is outside your control doesn't mean that you can relinquish responsibility for the stuff that is inside your control. Sometimes the search for answers requires some introspection.

So let's speak plainly. If you panicked and sold out of the markets at their market low it really does not matter if the price of gold changed by $10 in the last 30 days, or the Canadian dollar appreciated by a quarter of a cent, or if some corporation missed their profit estimates last quarter. It's all about you, and what you did.

If you can make the commitment to me to live within your means, add to your investments on a regular basis, load up on your investments when they periodically get cheap, and to stick to your long term plan... Well, if you can make that commitment to me, then I can do wonderful things for you.

But without that commitment it really doesn't matter what I do. Because what you do is going to overwhelm what I can do.

It's your own investor behaviour that matters. How much of your income do you put towards your financial objectives, and what do you do when the inevitable bear market starts growling.

Take responsibility for your own behaviours. Not everyone wants to hear that message. That doesn't make it any less true. And while not everyone is going to love me for saying it, I'd rather save you than please you.

From August 2012

Conclusion

MAKING GOOD FINANCIAL DECISIONS doesn't have to be impossibly hard. The good news is that if you do some simple things right, you can afford to have the occasional setback and still achieve prosperity. Here are some things to bear in mind which will significantly increase your odds of financial success.

- Hire a trusted, professional financial advisor. You don't know what you don't know.
- Live within your means.
- Spend some time thinking about what is really important in your life.
- Make decisions that are consistent with your objectives.
- When the narrative is no longer beneficial, just change the channel.
- It's not the iceberg that you see that sinks your ship; it's the one that you don't.
- All your hopes and dreams are reliant on continued good health, which is inherently unreliable. Protect your wealth from changes in your health.
- If you don't know where you are going, then any road will do.
- The number one fear for people heading into retirement is running out of money. You can greatly mitigate the risk of that happening with proper planning.

It's simple but it isn't always easy. Keep focused on your goals, make smart decisions with your money and you can achieve prosperity!

About the Author

Brad Brain, B.A. (Economics), CFP, R.F.P., CLU, CH.F.C, CHS, CIM, FCSI, TEP has been serving clients for more than 20 years with multi-disciplinary expertise. Brad is nationally recognized for retirement income planning. He is committed to helping his clients build multi-generational wealth through a prudent and disciplined approach to wealth creation and preservation.

What makes Brad unique is his strong protective instinct to keep his clients safe from harm. He can think creatively, communicate clearly, and keep focused on what is important, which has proven invaluable to cut through the cacophony of distractions and keep clients centered on what they need to do to achieve their financial and personal objectives.

www.bradbrainfinancial.com

About the Artwork

"Prosperity" is a five-panel acrylic painting commissioned by Brad Brain Financial Planning Inc, using many translucent layers of only 3 colours, white, azo gold, and pthalo blue, accented with hand-pulled rice paper printing and hand-carved blocks.

Koi fish represent prosperity and abundance in Eastern symbology. Nine koi rising to the pond surface represent a gathering of positive forces. Energy, in the form of a spiral, points to growth and change.

About the Artist

Barbara Daley is a mixed media artist working from her home studio, 7 Bangles Art & Design, in Fort St. John, in beautiful Northeastern British Columbia, Canada, on the Alaska Highway.

She is inspired by nature, travel, and by illustrating poetry, especially the Persian poets Rumi, Hafiz, and Kabir. Her favourite tools for expression are sketching and drawing on location, water media, acrylic painting, mixed media and textile art, Pan Pastels, meditative doodling, contemplative collage, photography and basic printmaking.

www.barbaradaleynearandfar.com